Y0-AAJ-928

libraries
in
france

Other comparative library studies

AUSTRALIAN LIBRARIES
by John Balnaves

CANADIAN LIBRARIES
by H C Campbell

HANDBOOK OF COMPARATIVE LIBRARIANSHIP
by S Simsova

LENIN, KRUPSKAIA & LIBRARIES
by S Simsova

NICHOLAS RUBAKIN & BIBLIOPSYCHOLOGY
by S Simsova

SOUTH AFRICAN LIBRARIES
by L E Taylor

libraries
in
france

JOHN FERGUSON MBE FLA

COMPARATIVE LIBRARY STUDIES

ARCHON BOOKS & CLIVE BINGLEY

FIRST PUBLISHED 1971 BY CLIVE BINGLEY LTD
THIS EDITION SIMULTANEOUSLY PUBLISHED IN THE USA
BY ARCHON BOOKS, THE SHOE STRING PRESS INC,
995 SHERMAN AVENUE, HAMDEN,
CONNECTICUT 06514
PRINTED IN GREAT BRITAIN
0 - 208 - 01058 - 0

Contents

	page
PREFACE	7
Chapter one THE FRENCH LIBRARY BOARD	9
Chapter two NATIONAL LIBRARIES WITH A NOTE ON COPY- RIGHT DEPOSIT	15
Chapter three PARIS, SOME MAJOR LIBRARIES	20
Chapter four PARIS, MUNICIPAL LIBRARIES	29
Chapter five PUBLIC LIBRARIES	34
Chapter six NON-MUNICIPAL GENERAL LIBRARIES	55
Chapter seven SCHOOL AND CHILDREN'S LIBRARIES	61
Chapter eight RURAL LIBRARIES : URBAN AND RURAL MOBILE SERVICES	69
Chapter nine UNIVERSITY LIBRARIES	77
Chapter ten LIBRARY METHODS	90
Chapter eleven INTER-LIBRARY COOPERATION	95
Chapter twelve THE LIBRARY PROFESSION; EDUCATION AND PROFESSIONAL ASSOCIATIONS	98
Chapter thirteen ARCHIVES AND DOCUMENTATION	106
Chapter fourteen THE PRESENT STATE OF LA LECTURE PUBLIQUE	110
INDEX	117

Preface

This book does not claim to be complete; it merely does what it can to summarise the current library situation in France.

It was inspired by the fact that the writer, on arrival in Paris to take up a library appointment, could not find a recent short description in English. Furthermore, after many visits to libraries of all kinds throughout the country, it became clear that French initiatives in municipal library practice, mobile libraries, library architecture and extension work were receiving scant attention in various recent international surveys. We all knew, it seemed, much more about conditions in Africa, India and the Far East than we did about the special problems of neighbouring France.

If more weight has been given to a consideration of community library affairs, it is because current difficulties cluster most thickly in this sector. In any case there are many excellent guides to the great national and learned libraries. Their treasures, like good wine, need no bush.

It is to be hoped that, as travel becomes commonplace, more and more librarians and scholars will visit France to see for themselves. I hope they will also make the acquaintance of the librarians, who deserve every possible sympathy and support as they campaign to make their library service truly worthy of the incomparable heritage of culture which is France.

The wealth of cathedrals, historic buildings and other evidences of an illustrious past, however, tends to conceal the fact that France is a young modern industrial power of great importance.

With about thirty two percent of its population under twenty years of age, it is becoming one of the youngest nations in Europe. Its population of about fifty million people is increasing steadily. As a producer of food, wine, cheese and other gastronomic delights its fame is universal. In textiles, steel, chemicals, electronics, motor vehicles, aircraft and light engineering its production is rising.

A forward-looking country, then, but one which retains an unforced respect for the past. In the special field of librarianship, however, one might suppose that this reverence had been carried to an extreme. In an altogether laudable attempt to preserve a superbly fine legacy of rare books and manuscripts, France has been slow in providing reading services for the nation as a whole. The separation of the *bibliothèque populaire* from the *bibliothèque savante* led to many difficulties.

The situation is now in process of being rectified, but the task is a heavy one. It has not been made any easier by the crisis in university education which, erupting in 1968, has proved to be difficult to resolve.

CHAPTER ONE

La Direction des Bibliothèques et de la Lecture Publique

Since the official title of the French Library Board is long, and since its name will appear often in the text, the contraction *Direction* will be used. The *Direction* is an official directorate of the *Ministère de l'Education Nationale*. As such it is the corner-stone of the French library movement and must remain its hope for the future. The head office is in Paris, in rue Lord Byron, near to the Avenue des Champs-Elysée.

The decree of the 19th August 1945, of the Provisional Government under General de Gaulle, which created the *Direction,* assigned three major tasks. They were:

Administration of the learned libraries;

Control of the municipal libraries;

Organisation and administration of *la lecture publique;* that is to say, reading facilities in the widest possible sense of the phrase.

Originally the title was simply *Direction des bibliothèques;* the addition was made to give added force to the board's interest in the public library sector. The present work of the *Direction* includes:

national libraries;
certain large specialised collections;
state university libraries;
municipal libraries;
rural libraries;
library education;
union catalogues;
inter-library co-operation;
the inspection of libraries.

9

1*

The Director of Libraries, who is also administrator of the National Library, is (1970) *M* Dennery, a distinguished civil servant and former ambassador of France. The current combination of the two posts is not necessarily a precedent. *M* Dennery is, of right, member of a number of important policy-making bodies. These include the *Conseil Supérieur de l'Education Nationale* and the *Conseil de l'Enseignment Supérieur*. He is also a permanent member of the *Comité National de la Documentation Scientifique et Technique*. The Director is well established in the appropriate corridors of power. He also has an active role to play as propagandist for library development, and speeches on the occasions of the inauguration of new projects provide valuable publicity.

Details of senior personnel and the main division of functions will be found in *Bottin administratif et documentaire,* or in the shorter annual *Répertoire permanent de l'administration française.*

The present Deputy Director is *M* Poindron, who is Inspector General of Libraries. He and his colleagues in the inspectorate have the task of evaluating the library services and of keeping contact with the librarians. Their reports draw attention to staff shortages, inadequate bookstocks and unsuitable premises.

The *Service Technique,* under its *Conservateur-en-Chef, M* Bleton, is involved if a library situation demands alterations, the enlargement of premises, or new structures. A staff of about six work on the planning, design, building construction, equipment and furniture aspects of the programme. The technical unit is interested not only on those libraries financed directly by the state, but equally in the independent municipal libraries which may, from time to time, qualify for state help. University library projects have demanded much attention in the years since 1945. More recently there has been a concentration of interest in the public library problems of France which affect both urban and rural communities and the *Service Technique* has worked out norms in connection with the provision of new community libraries.

There is a service of *Achats de Livres,* a centralised book-buying agency. It makes bulk purchases for the large group of *bibliothèques centrales de prêt* which serve the smaller urban and the rural communities, although acquisitions are also made for some municipal institutions.

A new section, *Lecture Publique,* was added to the *Direction* as a result of recommendations made in a report—*La lecture publique en France*—made in 1968. This surveyed the whole working of the library system, reported that it was in a critical condition, and made recommendations to bring about improvements. The task of the new unit is to initiate development in the public libraries, providing credits for additional staff and equipment. It is also closely concerned with the expansion of the *bibliobus,* or mobile library, services.

It will become evident, from succeeding pages, that the *Direction* has inherited a task of great magnitude. In addition to broad planning, it has to interest itself in the most minute details of library operation. Because of its central position it has had to establish uniform codes of practice.

During the second world war grave damage had been suffered by libraries in Caen, Strasbourg, Marseille and Paris. Elsewhere there had also been extensive damage to book stocks because of lack of heating and attention during the war years. The older universities in Montpellier, Lyon, Grenoble, Lille and Bordeaux were so overcrowded as to be unable to accommodate additional books, and Paris had many special problems because of the postwar rush of students to the university.

From its inception the *Direction* campaigned for a far-reaching plan of reconstruction, re-equipment and development, and demanded funds for the programme. In 1945 it presented, to a commission on needs in higher education, suggestions for a new large science library at the Halle aux Vins in Paris, as well as an extension to the Sainte-Geneviève and a new library of comparative law. In 1946 it reiterated its requirements in connection with the *Plan de Modernisation et d'Equipment,* the Monnet Plan. Attention was drawn to urgent needs in the Sorbonne library, the Sainte-Geneviève, the Law Faculty and the *Bibliothèque de Documentation Internationale Contemporaine* in Paris. Urgent provincial projects were listed at Aix-Marseilles, Besançon, Dijon, Grenoble, Montpellier, Rennes and Toulouse.

This move was unsuccessful but the demands were re-submitted in 1947 and 1948. In 1951 a *Commission du Plan d'Equipment Scholaire, Universitaire, Scientifique et Artistique* was established with the task of making a five year plan for educational development. M Julien Cain, then director, again drew attention to urgent library requirements and had these accepted. In this particular plan a subsequent decision limited expansion, but the *Direction* was able to apply its growing normal budget towards library development.

While examining and promoting such a programme, the *Direction* built up a store of technical expertise on buildings, construction, heating, ventilation, furniture, equipment and book supply which became of great value when the development began to accelerate. As funds, through the persistence of the *Direction,* became available, new equipment was provided in all university libraries, bulk purchases securing useful discounts.

In the meantime the career structure of the library profession had to be studied and regularised into official *statuts*. The sub-librarians in the technical grades were so organised in April 1950. The librarians themselves, and the separate group of *magasiniers,* or stack attendants, were given their *statut* in 1952. The *Direction* had then to set about raising the standards in library training for the various grades involved.

The numbers of staff employed, especially in the scientific grades, have been limited in comparison with levels in other developed countries. This fact has given point to the various codes of practice which the *Direction* has evolved since these not only result in operational economies but also facilitate the transfer and easy absorption of personnel moving from one service point to another.

In June 1962 new rules provided university libraries with a greater degree of open access. The cdu classification (udc) was recommended for use in all libraries other than those of medical faculties. Cataloguing procedures were agreed on and a standard lay-out of information on the catalogue card was adopted. A distinct division of library services was put into general use, this providing separate facilities for younger students.

The *Direction* has played a valuable role as a co-ordinator in projects which involve a wide range of general and special libraries. For example, in 1952 it created the *Catalogue collectif des ouvrages étangers,* a union catalogue of non-French works in French libraries. Another most useful initiative was the publication of the *Inventaire permanent des périodiques étrangers en cours;* a union catalogue of foreign periodicals which was first published in 1957. It assisted in the rapid build up of university scientific libraries through its *Service d'Information Bibliographique* which provided details of basic stock requirements. Through its periodicals it has tried to counter the isolation experienced by staff members working in remote libraries.

The monolithic aspect of the university library scene and certain standardised aspects of municipal and rural library administration may be surprising to those accustomed to the variety of methods to be encountered in other countries.

Since French librarians are as individualistic as the rest of us, and possibly more so, it is clear that the *Direction* must have proceeded with tact and discretion. The various problems were discussed at regular working conferences and agreement secured on possible solutions.

FURTHER READING

La lecture publique en France. La documentation française. (Notes et études documentaires no 3459 and reprinted in *Bulletin des bibiothèques de France,* March, 1968.) A basic document in the study of libraries in France.

Ministère de l'Education Nationale. Direction des Bibliothèques et de la Lecture Publique. Les bibliothèques de France au service du public. Paris, 1969. This is a most useful illustrated account of library services to young people, to general readers, to students, teachers and to research workers.

Masson, A and Salvan, P. *Les bibliothèques.* Paris, Presses Universitaires de France, 1963. Traces the history of the great libraries and gives an account of national, university, public and special services.

Recueil des textes législatifs concernant les bibliothèques, en vigeur au 1er mars 1954. Les bibliothèques relevant de la Direction des bibliothèques de France. Paris, Centre National de Documentation Pédagogique.

CHAPTER TWO

National libraries

The national libraries group in Paris (*La Réunion des Biblio-
thèques de Paris*) includes the following celebrated institutions:
Bibliothèque Nationale;
Bibliothèque de l'Arsenal;
Bibliothèque du Conservatoire;
Bibliothèque de l'Opéra.
The *Réunion* dates from 1926. At that time the *Sainte-
Geneviève* library was detached to become part of the University
of Paris libraries. The *Mazarine* library was detached from the
national libraries group in 1945 and attached to the *Institut de
France.* The group has its own budget and an administrative
council.

Three other libraries have administrative links with the *Bibliothèque Nationale.* These are the library of the Palace of Fontain-
bleau, the *Fondation-Smith-Lesouëf,* Nogent-sur-Marne, and the
storage depot of the BN at Versailles.
The National Library of France is, justly, regarded as one of
the world's most famous libraries. It is incontestably one of the
most elegant. It occupies a site of 16,500 square metres near to
the Bourse on the right bank of the Seine. It has enjoyed copyright facilities since 1537 in the domain of printed books. In
addition it possesses a very rich treasury of manuscripts, prints,
coins, medals and other records. Its current book holdings are in
the region of seven million volumes. Since there are so many
excellent accounts of the history of the library, it may be more
convenient to indicate, briefly, the main lines of its work and
to touch on current problems.
Under the Administrator General there are the following main
departments:

Printed books	Music
Periodicals	Maps and plans
Manuscripts	Copyright
Medals	Prints
Administration	

The legal deposit laws which have nurtured the great collection date from the *Ordonnance de Montpellier* of 1537.

Because of lack of space some of the departments have moved out of the main building to new premises. The music library is in a nearby location which also houses the state library school. Lesser-used books and periodicals are stored at Versailles and delivered by van when required. The stacks have been extended within the building. Space for readers, however, has long been strained to the limit. This makes the possibility of an extension a matter of vital importance, and use of the large central site recently vacated by the food markets of *Les Halles* has been mooted.

The case for a large reference annex to the BN is strong, since the city of Paris has no large central library, nor can the national library itself easily provide such a service. The projected library would be open to all, the accent being on current books and documents. It would also provide exhibition halls and conference rooms.

The project study for this extension is interesting since it meets many of the criticisms currently made of French libraries; to be specific, limited opening hours, insufficient space for readers and a restrictive attitude towards users. The building would provide the following main areas:

reading and documentation	11,000 square metres approx
exhibition space	1,000 ,, ,,
meeting rooms	900 ,, ,,
public rooms	1,500 ,, ,,

Other statistics:

eventual stock	1,000,000 volumes
reading room seats	1,300 approx
daily ' entries '	3,000 to 4,000 visitors
hours	10.00 hrs to 22.00 hrs daily including Sundays

It would not be a lending library, but it is hoped that the city of Paris would make lending facilities available nearby. There would be a strong periodicals collection, and a comprehensive bibliographical unit would also be provided. To permit rapid internal movement escalators would be preferable to elevators. Computer facilities would be available, and the total library staff would be two hundred.

In turning again to the existing considerable resources of the national libraries, the *Bibliothèque de l'Arsenal* is noteworthy. Founded in 1757 by the Marquis de Paulmy, it is especially rich in literature, art and history. It enjoys copyright deposit facilities in the field of literary texts of which there are many special collections of outstanding value. It has an unrivalled collection of theatrical archives.

The *Conservatoire National de Musique,* founded in 1795, has large resources of material on ancient and contemporary music though its copyright deposits are more recent and date from 1925. It also collects all books on music and all musical scores. In 1935 it joined the national libraries group.

The library of the Paris *Opéra* dates from 1866 and specialises in operatic music, stage design, theatrical costume and related topics.

Although not in the Paris group of national libraries, the *Bibliothèque Nationale et Universitaire* of Strasbourg has national status and ranks next to the *Bibliothèque Nationale*. It has had a chequered career, and its proximity to the German border involved it in many conflicts. It suffered extensive damage in the second world war. It has a special place in the classification of the libraries of France since it is at the same time regional centre for Alsace-Lorraine, city library for Strasbourg, and also the university library with extensive specialised collections in the fields of medicine, science and technology.

COPYRIGHT DEPOSIT

Legal deposit is regulated by law no 341 of the 21st June 1943. This requires the deposit of copies of books, periodicals, brochures, prints, engravings, illustrated postcards, notices, maps, musical works and photographs. Invitation cards, visiting cards and other similar items are excluded.

Publishers must submit four copies, before sales and circulation, to the *Bibliothèque Nationale*. In addition, a copy must be sent to the Ministry of the Interior.

There are separate instructions for printers. They must send two copies to the *Bibliothèque Nationale*, if they print in the Paris area. For the reception of items printed outside Paris there are nineteen classified libraries which are empowered, under article 5 of the law, to receive printed materials. These regional holders of copyright materials are in Amiens, Angers, Besançon, Bordeaux, Châlons-sur-Marne, Clermont-Ferrand, Dijon, Lille, Limoges, Lyon, Marseille, Montpellier, Nancy, Orléans, Poitiers, Rennes, Rouen, Strasbourg (*Bibliothèque Nationale et Universitaire*), and Toulouse.

Special rules apply to *de luxe* editions with restricted print runs. In the case of music, while the publisher is required to fulfil his obligations, the printer need not submit copies.

Free postal facilities are provided.

Independently of these requirements, publications directed at young people are controlled by a law of 16th July 1949. Five copies must be deposited at the Ministry of Justice.

FURTHER READING

Cain, J: *Les transformations de la BN, 1930-36.* BN, 1936.

Esdaile, A: *National libraries of the world.* Library Association, second edition 1957.

Foncin, M: ' Les nouvelles installations du département des cartes et plans de la BN '. Assn des Bibliothécaires Française *Bulletin d'informations.* 15, November 1954.

La Bibliothèque Nationale: *La documentation française illustrée.* No 244. February 1969.

Ledos, E G: *Histoire des catalogues imprimés de la BN.* BN, 1936.

Raport sur le fonctionnement des divers services de la BN. 1933 and 1934. Issued 1936.

1945 to 1951. Issued 1954.

1952 to 1955. Issued 1958. (These are official BN reports.)

Seguin, J-P: *Le service des magazines de la salle de travail du département des imprimés.* BN, 1960.

Seguin, J P: 'La bibliothèque des Halles'. ABF *Bulletin d'informations* 62(1) 1969.

CHAPTER THREE

Some major libraries in Paris

La Bibliothèque Sainte-Geneviève occupies a special place in the system, and indeed in the affections of all who know it. It was, as we have seen, in the group of national libraries from 1926 to 1930 and retains substantial copyright deposit facilities. It receives all the *dépôt légale d'imprimeur* items except in music, art and literature, and is currently one of the most important units of the University of Paris libraries. At the same time it retains its centuries-old functions as a general public library, welcoming scholars and readers with a minimum of formality.

The collection was started in the Middle Ages in the Abbey of Sainte-Geneviève which became a seat of learning. The early stocks of books were dispersed but, reformed by Louis XIII in 1619, it was re-founded. A large donation of 16,000 choice books was made by Cardinal Le Tellier in 1710 which doubled the collection and gave it rank second only to the Royal Library. Under the Revolution it was nationalised, in 1790, and took the name *Bibliothèque du Pantheón*. Since its inception it had been fortunate to have vigorous librarians. Under the Directory this luck continued. Its head, Danou, had the pick of the confiscated collections, not only of France but of Europe. In addition he instituted a regular programme of purchases with a government grant. In 1815, under the Restoration, it resumed its familiar title and in 1844 to 1850 it obtained its present buildings facing the Place du Panthéon.

From its inception it had occupied various rooms in the abbey, eventually having a very fine gallery. For its new home Henri Labrouste designed a functional building of great charm. The iron-frame structure was left undisguised to become a decorative feature of the very large reading room. The long wall facing the

Panthéon was left fairly solid and unnecessary windows were not permitted to interfere with book storage requirements.

The book collection is encyclopedic. It is especially rich in the fields of theology, canon law, law generally and history. There are about 1,250 early printed books and special collections of manuscripts and rare bindings. There are many special collections built up by the long line of librarians, and the modern collections total about one million volumes.

It has two special libraries. These are the *Bibliothèque Finno-Scandinave* and the *Jacques-Doucet* library. The first assembles books and periodicals dealing with the Nordic countries and was founded in 1868. The *Bibliothèque Littéraire Jacques-Doucet* is devoted to contemporary literature and to those nineteenth century writers who influenced its development. The library has a large collection of literary reviews.

The libraries of the University of Paris comprise a group of some twenty general and special collections. Many of these are in the densely settled fifth *arrondissement*, which is the traditional home of the university. However, the continuing rapid growth in student numbers has led to the creation of very large establishments on the outskirts of the city. The problem will be discussed in chapter nine.

The centrepiece of the group is the *Sorbonne* library. This was founded in the celebrated college of theology instituted by Robert de Sorbon in 1253. Towards the end of the sixteenth century the college became the nucleus of the University of Paris. Its very rich collections of early books and manuscripts are of a general nature. The modern holdings are in the fields of science and the humanities. Particularly well represented are history, philosophy, theology, archaeology, mathematics, physics, chemistry and the natural sciences.

Because of the wealth of the collections the Sorbonne library is very much a research library for scholars and advanced students. The newer university libraries in, for example, the *Centre Censier* and at Nanterre, Orsay and Vincennes, are able to relate their holdings more directly to the teaching programmes and to the special needs of the mass of undergraduate students.

The *Bibliothèque de documentation internationale contemporaine* (BDIC), is an important unit in the university group. It was originally the library of the *Musée de la Guerre* and was given to the state in 1917. Heavy losses were suffered when its premises in Vincennes caught fire at the time of the liberation of Paris in 1944. It has, nevertheless, a wealth of material on the 1871-1914 period and the 1914-1918 years are similarly well documented. The period of the second world war and afterwards includes material on British, American, Italian, Russian and German involvement.

BDIC takes as its main task the documentation of political, economic and social problems arising out of national and international relations.

The university group includes the well known libraries of the faculties of law, medicine, and pharmacy. These libraries and the *Bibliothèque d'Art et d'Archéologie* are dealt with on subsequent pages. In addition there are over fifty institute or laboratory libraries covering a very wide range of subjects from aviation to town planning.

The library of the *Institut de France* dates from 1795. Its original collections were made by Antoine Moriau who eventually bequeathed them to the city of Paris. At the time, the various learned academies were gathered together under the title *Institut de France* and given space in the *Collège Mazarin*. It benefited largely from the books stored in the *dépôts littéraires,* as a result of revolutionary confiscations. Over the years, too, the members of the academies have made many donations. In 1825 the printed books totalled 70,000 volumes. In 1950 the figure was $1\frac{1}{2}$ millions, to which must be added large collections of brochures, periodicals and manuscripts.

ART LIBRARIES

Paris is well endowed in this subject. The city has its own extensive collection in the Forney library, which is specially strong in industrial design and related topics.

The University of Paris administers the *Bibliothèque d'Art et d'Archaeologie*. This large specialised collection is of great value to students of the history of art. In addition to the extensive collection of books there are notable libraries of prints and photographs. The original collections were made by Jacques Doucet; initially they were made available to the public in his own house, but in 1918 they were donated to the university.

Another private foundation is dedicated to graphic art—the *Bibliothèque des Arts Graphiques*. The library was founded in 1930 by Edmond Morin. It is now in the care of the city of Paris.

Other noteworthy art libraries are:

Conservatoire National des Arts et Métiers;

École Nationale Supérieure des Arts Décoratif;

École Nationale Supérieure des Beaux-Arts;

Manufacture Nationale des Gobelins;

Union Centrale des Arts Décoratifs.

ETHNOGRAPHY, ETHNOLOGY

The key collection in this field is in the *Musée de l'Homme* in the Palais de Chaillot on the high ground overlooking the Champ de Mars and the Eiffel Tower. It specialises in physical anthropology, human paleontology, prehistory and ethnography.

The original library was built up from 1880 onwards in the *Musée d'Ethnographie du Trocadére*. In 1937 the museum took its present name and moved into its new home. At the same time the range was widened. Various specialised ethnological and other societies made their book and periodicals collections available while retaining ultimate possession. In this way materials on Africa, America, and other regions were added, as were books on pre-history and archeology. The various society collections were arranged in one systematic sequence; the library uses the Library of Congress classification scheme.

In addition to the extensive book collection there is a periodicals collection and a library of sound recordings of the music and song of various ethnic groups. The photographic library contains over 200,000 items. The library is freely open to the public, though loans from duplicate volumes are restricted to approved students.

French ethnography is collected in the *Musée des Arts et Traditions Populaires*. This consists of books, periodicals, archives, maps, manuscripts, and sound recordings.

GRANDES ÉCOLES

Although the *Grandes écoles* train only one student in twenty in France in the field of higher education, nevertheless, their prestige is enormous. Their ex-students are to be found everywhere in the upper reaches of administration, engineering and industry.

The library of the *École Polytechnique* is representative. It is specially strong in the sciences—mathematics, astronomy, physics, biology, pure and applied science. Founded in 1794, its aim is to train civil and military engineers. It is under the control of the War Ministry.

Other libraries in this group are:

École Normale Supérieure (1795);
École Nationale Supérieure des Mines (1794);
École Nationale des Chartes (1821);
École Nationale des Langues Orientales Vivantes (1795);
Fondation Nationale des Sciences Politiques (1871);
École Nationale Supérieure des Beaux-Arts (1864).

HISTORY

The national library, the Arsenal and the Sainte-Geneviève are all of great importance in this field.

The opportunity is taken, however, of drawing attention to one of the richest collections in all France, that of the *Bibliothèque Mazarine*. This originated in the personal library of Cardinal Mazarin and was open to scholars from 1643 onwards. In this way it can claim to be the oldest public library in the country. It was one of the national libraries until 1945, at which date it was attached to the *Institut de France*.

The library enjoys copyright deposit rights. Its older collections are rich in books on philosophy and history; these two subjects are also strongly represented in current publications. There are also many manuscripts and rare books.

Other sources for historical materials are:
Bibliothèque Historique de la Ville de Paris;
Archives Nationales;
Archives de la Seine;
Musée de l'Armée.

LAW AND POLITICAL ECONOMY

Paris provides many sources for materials on law and politics. In the university group the libraries of the Law faculty and that of the *Sainte-Geneviève* are good starting points. Other libraries are:
Fondation Nationale des Sciences Politiques;
Chambre de Commerce de Paris;
Bibliothèque de la Direction de la Documentation;
Bibliothèque de la France d'Outre-Mer;
Bibliothèque de Documentation Internationale Contemporaine;
Institut Scientifique de Recherches Economiques et Sociales;
Institut de Statistique de l'Université de Paris;
Institut National de la Statistique et des Etudes Economiques (INSEE);
Maison de Science de l'Homme.

Medical libraries are dealt with in chapter nine, on university libraries.

MUSIC

The Department of Music of the *Bibliothèque Nationale* is an obvious source. It has very large resources on ancient music. The library of the Paris Opera, Place Charles Garnier, specialises in operatic music, stage design and the history of costume. The library of the *Conservatoire National de Musique* has collections which range from ancient to contemporary music, and much material on composers. The three libraries above share copyright materials on music.

Other libraries with specialised collections are:
Institut de Musicologie de l'Université de Paris;

25

Bibliothèque Centrale Musicale of ORTF (the French TV and radio organisation);
Société des Auteurs et Compositeurs Dramatiques;
Centre de Documentation de Musique Internationale.

NATURAL HISTORY

The largest source in this field is the central library of the *Muséum National d'Histoire Naturelle.* It is another example of a great scientific institution with an illustrious past. It has been in existence since 1635 and was part of the *Cabinet du Jardin du Roi.* At the time of the revolution it received many additional books from the confiscations. A decree of 1793 gave the library its present name and it became the first great public library to be founded from the stocks of confiscated books. These came chiefly from Notre-Dame and the other ecclesiastical collections, to which were added duplicates from the *Bibliothèque Nationale.*

Among the treasures of the library are the paintings on vellum of rare plants in the garden, at Blois, of the Duke of Orléans. These date from about 1640. The library is administered by the *Direction.*

PARLIAMENTARY AND MINISTERIAL LIBRARIES

Members of parliament have their own elegant working library in the *Assemblée Nationale.* This is a large general collection with special reference to legislation, receiving all French administrative publications under *dépôt légale* arrangements. It has built up, since 1932, a busy documentation centre on administration and related topics. The Library possesses a rich store of early books, manuscripts and documents. Founded in 1796, it was installed in its present quarters, which have decorations by Delacroix, in 1840.

An equally rich collection is provided in the Luxembourg Palace—the library of the *Conseil de la République.* Though this is a general collection, it is predominantly concerned with law, economics, administration and history, as well as having long runs of parliamentary papers. Like the *Assemblée Nationale* it is reserved for members. The library dates from 1860.

There are numerous ministerial libraries in Paris. Some of these are restricted to government personnel as is the case in the large library of the *Ministère des Affaires Etrangères*. On the other hand, some ministerial collections are reserved ' *en principe* ' for internal use, but they may be disposed to offer facilities to approved readers, one example of this being the library of the *Ministère de l'Agriculture*.

Some of the principal ministerial libraries are:
Ministère de l'Education Nationale, Direction de l'Architecture;
Ministère des Finances;
Ministère de l'Industrie et du Commerce;
Ministère de l'Intérieur;
Ministère de la Reconstruction et de l'Urbanisme;
Ministère de la Santé Publique;
Ministère du Travail.

GRAMOPHONE RECORD LIBRARIES

The national collection of recordings was first started in 1911. In 1938 this became, officially, the *Phonothèque Nationale* as a branch of the national library and with copyright deposit rights. The library has two tasks: that of receiving the copyright records, and also that of conserving related documents and equipment. It encountered many difficulties in the second world war and it was not always able to secure copies of discs issued. The build up of records was:

1938-1953   17,586 discs deposited
1954-1958   21,064   ,,   ,,
1959-1963   31,801   ,,   ,,

Since then the annual production has been in the region of 7,500 discs. Tape recordings are also collected and there are many recordings by famous French citizens. Folklore is well represented. There is a library of books on sound recordings and a museum of early sound equipment as well as a laboratory which can be used to copy recordings. In 1963 it came under the care of the *Direction*. The 1966 staff totalled eighteen plus three part time staff. In 1965 the *Phonothèque* moved to larger premises in rue Louvois where it has 911 square metres of working space.

The record requirements of the ORTF are served by its own well equipped *Discothèque Centrale*.

Other record and tape libraries will be found in many of the specialised institutions of Paris. The following are worthy of mention:

Musée de l'Homme;
Musée des Arts et Traditions Populaires;
Musée Guimet;
Centre de Documentation Musicale Internationale;
Centre National de Documentation Pédagogique.

Parisians may make use of the collections in the *Discothèque de Paris* through certain city libraries, though minors require an authorisation from a parent or teacher. The type of playing head used in the borrower's record player is first verified. In addition to the libraries currently served, the *Discothèque de Paris* has plans to develop gramophone record collections in other city libraries. Established in 1966, it issued 114,347 records in 1969.

FURTHER READING

Répertoire des bibliothèques de France. Bibliothèques de Paris UNESCO/*Direction des Bibliothèques.* 1950. Though, fortunately, dated this is an indispensable list of libraries. It sets out, most clearly, the history and administrative arrangements in each institution.

Bonnerot, J: *L'ancienne Université de Paris, centre international d'études.* Paris, 1928.

Burton, M and Esdaile, A: *Famous libraries of the world.* Grafton, 1937.

Decollogne, R: 'La Phonothèque Nationale'. *Bulletin des bibliothèques de France,* February 1967.

Duprat, G: 'La bibliothèque du Muséum National d'Histoire Naturelle'. *Bulletin des Bibliothèques de France,* January 1965.

Discothèque de Paris. 1969 report. Paris, 1970.

Franklin: *Les anciennes bibliothèques de Paris.* Paris, 1867-1873.

Serrurier, C: *Bibliothèques de France; description de leur fonds et historique de leur formation.* La Haye, Nijhoff, 1946.

CHAPTER FOUR

Paris municipal libraries

The municipal libraries of Paris currently lend over three million books each year. This works out at 1.1 per inhabitant served and is above the national average. It should be noted that the area referred to is the city of Paris and not the much larger unit of *le District de la Region Parisienne* which takes in the whole area of the conurbation. Another factor which should be taken into account is the very high population density of the city, being about 114 people per acre, compared with forty five in London.

Paris is divided into twenty *arrondissements,* each of which has four *quartiers.* The present library provision is:

20   *arrondissement* or ' central ' libraries;
53   *quartier* libraries, mostly in school buildings;
3   children's libraries;
9   libraries in youth clubs;
    La bibliothèque Forney (textiles, design, fine arts);
    La bibliothèque Marguerite Durand (feminism);
    La bibliothèque historique de la Ville de Paris.

As has been noted, in connection with the reference on the proposed extension of the National Library, Paris lacks a large central library.

The ensemble above is not part of the *Direction des Bibliothèques* group, but is controlled by the city council under the direction of the *Chef du Bureau des Bibliothèques de la Préfecture de la Seine.* Paris, unlike other French municipalities, has no mayor. The Préfet of the Seine region is the state official in charge of city affairs.

Paris set up its first *arrondissement* library in 1865. Previously there had been efforts, along the lines of the mechanics' institutes, to provide libraries for working men. A lithographer, M Girard established a *Société des Amis de l'Instruction* in 1837 which had a library financed by members. It was the mayor of the eleventh *arrondissement* who gathered a collection of 800 books and put forward the idea of a free library with a staff dedicated to the task of encouraging readers. He secured a grant-in-aid from the city in 1838 and after this his lead was followed in other parts of the city. In 1879, the préfet, M Herold, not only founded ten new libraries but gathered the existing ones into a *Service Central des Bibliothèques* in order that the widely varying methods should be standardised. The city provided further funds for development and in the period from 1879 to 1902 no less than seventy new libraries opened in addition to the introduction of lending for home reading. Sample book circulation figures were:

1879   57,840
1901   2,046,209
1914   1,148,983.

The drop in transactions was ascribed to the fact that worn out books were not being replaced. Readers were repelled by the poor physical state of the stock and the absence of up to date reading matter. The books were often kept in locked cupboards; the part time librarians were not trained, were poorly paid and had little interest in their work.

In 1941 the system was reformed. Ten of the *arrondissement* libraries were put on a full time basis. The readers returned and issue figures rose again. Full time opening in this context means about forty hours of service per week. The schedule was applied to the larger units with lending, reference and children's libraries. The small libraries in the *salles de quartier* generally offer a restricted service of about seven hours per week.

Most of the 'central' libraries were allocated space in the *mairies*. Economies in running expenses resulted, since heating, lighting and supervision expenses were thus shared. However, this approach meant that possibilities of expansion were often ruled out.

The library service is free; those who register present their identity cards. Gramophone record libraries have an initial subscription of F5 and subscribers pay one franc a week for each record borrowed.

Open access methods have been in use for more than fifty years. A notice published in October, 1914, reads:
'*Avis aux lecteurs. Libre accès des rayons.*

La faculté donnée aux lecteurs d'accéder librement aux rayons, comme en Angleterre, est de nature à deculper l'utilité de la Bibliothèque . . . Le libre accès exige du public une discipline volontaire indispensable . . .'

The city has a programme designed to rehouse many of the overcrowded libraries, although sites are difficult to find in a city as densely settled as Paris.

The library of the sixth *arrondissement* in rue Bonaparte is an example of a recent complete modernisation of an existing library. From 1881 onwards it had been allocated a first floor room of modest dimensions. The growing collections eventually restricted reading room places. Only a dozen or so readers could be accommodated in a space quite crowded with bookshelves, catalogue cabinets, tables and the issue desk. The refurbished library is on the ground floor. One of the large ceremonial halls of the mairie has been converted with great taste and the height of the room permits the use of a two tier stack which remains fully open to the public. The gallery provides additional public space. Provision is also made for a periodicals lounge, a children's library and, in addition to the normal lending and reference facilities, a gramophone record collection with an initial stock of 1,500 discs.

The *Bibliothèque-discothèque* of the eighteenth *arrondissement* is an example of recent new construction. It was opened in November 1967 to replace a central library which had only one table for users of reference books and which crowded all its activities into an area of ninety square metres. The new lending library alone provides 460 square metres of space. The stacks occupy the first floor and there is a reading-room on the second. The gramophone record library is extensive and a room is provided for concerts of recorded music (100 seats).

The Forney library (*Bibliothèque Municipale d'Art et d'Industrie Forney*) is a large collection which specialises in industrial design, art, crafts and associated subjects. It has a specially rich collection of prints, lithographs, plans, models and fabrics—the celebrated ' *toiles de Jouy* '. In addition to reference services there are home-lending facilities. The library was founded, as the result of a donation by M Aimé-Samuel Forney, in 1886. Its object was to provide technical assistance to artisans, to elevate standards in industrial design and to improve contacts between industrialists, businessmen and workers. In 1928 the library was rehoused in the former palace of the archbishop of Sens.

Another town house in the Marais, the *Hôtel de Lamoignon* was saved from destruction and renovated with great care to house the extensive local collection of the city. *La bibliothèque Historique de la Ville de Paris* had its new installations inaugurated in January 1969. Its book resources have grown from 100,000 in 1898 to about 400,000 in 1968. 5,700 volumes on Paris history are on open access in the reading-room. There are valuable collections of periodicals and manuscripts. In addition to about 120 early printed books, the library has more than one thousand sixteenth century books and an impressive collection of rare bindings. It is specially strong in maps of the city and of the Ile-de-France. The poster collection includes revolutionary notices, occupation instructions and street posters relating to the events of 1968.

One of the city's special collections is devoted to feminism. The *Bibliothèque Marguerite-Durand* is composed entirely of books, documents, photographs and press cuttings on the history of women's rights. The original collection was assembled by Marguerite Durand who presented the materials to the city in 1932. Space was found in the *mairie* of the fifth *arrondissement*.

FURTHER READING

Bulletin de la Société des Amis de la Bibliothèque Forney (quarterly).

Carnovsky, L: ' Public libraries of Paris '. *Library quarterly* XXII (3) 1952.

Clarke, J A: ' French libraries in transition, 1789-95 '. *Library quarterly* XXXVII (4) 1967.

Coeytaux, V: 'Le centenaire des bibliothèques municipales parisiennes'. *Bulletin des bibliothèques de France*, February 1966.

Surirey de Saint-Remy, H: 'La Bibliothèque Historique de la Ville de Paris'. *Bulletin des bibliothèques de France*, February 1969.

CHAPTER FIVE

Public libraries

Metropolitan France has ninety five *départements*. A decree of 1959 created twenty economic regions to take care of overall planning. The *départements* are in turn divided into approximately:

310   *arrondissements*

3,030   *cantons*

38,000 *communes.*

The last-named, the *commune* is the unit of local government. While it may attain a considerable size, as in Marseille, most are limited in population. In 1954, no less than 34,000 of the 38,000 units had fewer than 1,500 inhabitants. Clearly the existence of such a large number of small, independent communities poses difficult administrative problems.

The *maire* is not only chief citizen but also chief executive. He is subject only to the authority of the *préfet,* the high-ranking government official who presides over the larger local government machine in the *département.*

Municipal financial powers are limited. They are further afflicted by the decline in the rural population. There is a fairly large scale movement towards the cities. However, the *commune* tends to cling tenaciously to its independence and is not always responsive to the wishes of the central authorities. The local mayor presides over the affairs of his own library and he may also play a part in the affairs of the rural library service, the *Bibliothèque centrale de prêt* which may serve the area.

The earliest town library, that of Lyon, was founded in 1530, and several other municipal libraries had been set up by the time of the French revolution. At this period collection points were established in Paris and other centres for the purpose of storing the large stocks of books and manuscripts previously owned by the religious houses and the noble families. These confiscations were allocated to various municipalities where they were to be made accessible to all.

Many municipal libraries date, therefore, from this period and began life with, in some cases, considerable stocks of rare books. On closer inspection, however, the religious, philosophical and other treatises held little appeal for their new owners. Nor were the collections kept alive by sizeable new additions to stock. In many cases, indeed, the confiscations were ' devoured by the dust ', stolen, or sold off by weight to make room for other municipal activities.

Where the work of conservation had been carried out with more devotion and better success, the collections began to attract the notice of scholars. From 1830 onwards there was a steady growth in the use of municipal libraries by those engaged in historical studies. At about this period, therefore, the national patrimony of ancient records gave to the French municipal library the character of a *bibliothèque d'étude* for the leisured and cultivated few; a concept which has tended to persist.

At present there are fifty *bibiothèques classées* or classified libraries. According to a recent report on the library service, there are 600 municipal libraries, and nearly 700 if one includes those in Paris.

All municipal libraries are inspected by the *Direction,* and qualify for grants towards reorganisation and new projects. The list of classified libraries is related to the comparative wealth of their stock of rare books. In such institutions the *personnel scientifique,* that is to say, the chief librarian and perhaps one or two colleagues, are members of the state corps of librarians. Other staff members are local municipal officers. To some extent the state librarian is present to ensure that all is well with the treasury of rare books.

More recently, however, the absolute necessity to activate the service has become the dominant factor in shaping policy. The word ' animation ' is therefore popular and the traditionalist approach is regarded with suspicion.

It must not be assumed that the best progress is to be observed in the larger systems. Many smaller ' unclassified ' systems have recently made excellent progress. One could quote St-Dié in the Vosges, with 25,000 inhabitants. Library use is here developing rapidly and there is a very full calendar of extension activities. Recent results are:

1960 16,000 books issued
1969 181,000 books issued
     6,000 gramophone records issued
     4,827 members.

The list of classified systems is as follows:

Aix-en-Provence	Dijon	Nice
Albi	Dole	Nîmes
Amiens	Douai	Orléans
Angers	Grenoble	Pau
Avignon	La Rochelle	Périgueux
Besançon	Le Havre	Poitiers
Bordeaux	Le Mans	Rheims
Boulogne-sur-mer	Lille	Rennes
Brest	Limoges	Rouen
Bourges	Lyon	Saint-Etienne
Caen	Marseille	Toulouse
Cambrai	Metz	Tours
Carpentras	Montpellier	Troyes
Châlons-sur-Marne	Moulins	Valence
Clermont-Ferrand	Mulhouse	Valenciennes
Colmar	Nancy	Versailles
Compiègne	Nantes	

Since it is impossible to comment on all of the classified libraries, a few short descriptions are added to establish the basic patterns of municipal library development. Where special features are to be found, these are indicated.

Besançon is an example of a town in which the *conservateur* of the municipal library is also the university librarian. The arrangement was made in the early days of the university's development. The municipal library has a very large book-stock; additional stacks have been built inside the existing reading rooms, reducing working space for readers to an absolute minimum. There is a separate 'popular' lending library, which is also supported by the *commune*. While the arrangement tends to separate physically research workers, university students and general readers, it encourages a very useful rationalisation of the book selection policy for the town.

Bordeaux (population 283,528) has a large city system with twelve lending libraries and two mobile libraries. Its central library has been reorganised. In 1963 a 300-seat reading room opened, in 1964 a new stack was built and in 1966 a catalogue hall with a wide range of bibliographical aids was added. Lending services open to the public from 9.00-12.00 and from 15.00-19.00 hours on normal working days. Lending is free to children. Adults pay F1.50 per quarter and may borrow two books at a time.

Caen (population 95,000) suffered extensive damage in the Normandy landings during the second world war. While it yet lacks a proper central library it is developing attractive branches and there is a *bibliobus* service to six suburbs. A new 5,000 square metre central library is being constructed. Block loans are made to youth clubs. The children's libraries are well used and welcoming. In the programme of activities one finds story hours, puppet shows, gramophone record recitals and slide projection programmes. Membership fees are:

under 15   F1 annually

15-18   F2

adults   F5

Cambrai (35,000) is another town in which unpromising quarters have been resourcefully extended and developed into a thriving library service with much emphasis on cultural activities. The library coordinates the work of the various groups and publishes a monthly programme. In common with Caen, Tours and some other busy municipal libraries loans are recorded on tape, since this method has proved to be less costly than photo-charging. Cambrai's plans for the future include a large extension of lending services and an auditorium for theatrical performances and other functions. A 1,370 square metre extension is featured in the 1970 building programme.

Clermont-Ferrand (135,000) has a library system which unites town and gown. The original municipal system dates from 1742 and acquired large stocks at the period of the revolution. The university library, which dates from 1880, comes under the control of the municipal librarian, as in Besançon. The university and city libraries have a combined stock of 400,000 volumes. In addition to these specialised services there is a municipal *bibliothèque populaire* with 16,000 volumes, or less than ·1 per head. The lending membership fee is F5 per annum. It attracts 2·25 percent of the city population. There are some deposit stations and an urban mobile library. There is a separate children's library, *L'Heure Joyeuse.*

Colmar (52,000). Since there were many rich religious houses in the upper Rhine country, Colmar is heir to a very distinguished collection of rare books and manuscripts. Its *conservateur* is also in charge of the rich museum of religious art for which the town is famous. The needs of ordinary reading have not, however, been forgotten; plans have been made to extend the lending library and the service to young readers.

Grenoble (165,202) is one of the most dynamic of French cities. Its new industries are expanding and the increase in population has been rapid. The city authorities have, since 1945, opened eight branch libraries. In 1956 it inaugurated France's first urban *bibliobus.* Its library expenditure is well above the general level and has steadily increased:

Year	Population	Total expenditure in francs	Percentage of total municipal budget	Cost per head in francs
1959	111,371	424,080	·76	3·81
1965	162,764	1,054,911	1·48	6·48
1969	165,202	1,835,135	1·45	11·11

Le Havre (185,553). For a full account of this attractive central library inaugurated in 1967 see the *Bulletin des bibliothèques de France* (July 1968). Its plate glass windows allowing clear views of the interior are a welcome sign of a new approach in planning.

The provision of work space in the stack area ' for certain privileged readers ' is similarly a break with tradition.

Lille (194,948). A guide to the city published in 1772 drew the attention of visitors to the existence of a well-chosen and rich library. At the time of the first world war, it was in the town hall. This was destroyed by fire in 1916. Those books which could be saved were taken to the university library. The new municipal library, opened in 1965, is an extremely pleasant, modern building which caters for a full range of general and special services.

The stack building is on nine levels and can hold about 500,000 books. The lending library has approximately 13,000 volumes, but the city has, of course, various branches.

A large exhibition gallery is provided. The reading room has places for about 140 readers and the periodicals room can accommodate about thirty people. The children's library has shelf space for about 4,000 books and can receive fifty children. Space is provided for activities and story hours.

Much attention has been paid to the functional aspects of the building, with the possibility of an eventual extension being considered. The foundations are capable of carrying three additional stack floors. The part of the building facing the street, which houses the public departments, can be extended upwards by one floor.

Lyon (535,000) has a municipal library with a long and distinguished history. The city library originated about 1530 in a religious college which passed into the hands of the Jesuits. The collection grew as a result of purchases and bequests, though during the revolution much damage was caused to the library.

In spite of its turbulent history, however, Lyon is celebrated in that it has the richest collection of manuscripts in any of the provincial libraries. There are 10,000 of these and over 1,000 incunables and 20,000 prints.

The book stock is particularly rich in sixteenth and seventeenth century works and in eighteenth century books on science. Among the special libraries in the municipal network is a museum of printing in a seventeenth century town house presented to the city by the *Credit Lyonnais.*

Lyon is a thriving industrial city, being the centre of a very large conurbation and has a network of library branches. A new central library is under construction on a 5,000 square metre site in the city. The emphasis will be on an informal service for the general reader. This project for a new public library in Lyon is the largest yet undertaken by the *Direction* in the public library field.

Marseille (893,711) is second largest city in France and a commercial, maritime and cultural centre of importance. It possesses a network of municipal library branches and a mobile library service for the urban areas. However, its central library is miserably overcrowded in an unsuitable building in Place Auguste Carli, though a replacement central library has been planned. This will provide two very large reading rooms, a lending section, a children's library, a gramophone record library and a special room for the consultation of rare books and other restricted materials. The stack will be large and there will be space for the library's regional copyright activities and for a bindery.

Mulhouse (118,558) decided to reorganise its ' popular libraries ' by modernising the various premises and by removing the older accumulations of reference works. Daily opening schedules were instituted in the various branch libraries and the annual closure during the month of August was discontinued. In 1968 the membership rates were increased sixty six percent; lending fee to F6, reference facilities to F10. This tended to hold back the membership increase. Mulhouse libraries register 6·1 percent of the city population, but they also attract users from 134 neighbouring *communes* and from sixteen other communities in the Mulhouse *agglomération*. The city had been anxious to improve its services for some time. It was one of the first libraries to benefit from the 1968 additions to the funds of the *Direction*. The central government grants permitted large additions to stock, provided a mobile library and assisted the branch development programme. The effect of the assistance on purchases can be judged by the following table:

	1967 F (millions)	1968 F (millions)
Municipal budget	110·1	161·9
Ministry of Education grant	—	47·4
Total	110·1	209·3

Tours (112,560) is the home of one of France's most successful library services. The central library is well housed in a modern building and there is a great deal of emphasis placed on the idea that the library should be the centre for cultural activities. The lending services are particularly well developed; a ' theme for the month ' encourages readers to widen their interests. Special facilities exist for teenagers, in addition to a children's library which runs a variety of extension projects. There is a special collection of American books, Tours being the American university centre for European studies. The exhibition galleries are extensive. Rooms are provided for meetings of learned societies and the auditorium provides facilities for concerts and other functions. Like other major municipal libraries it has a programme for the in-service training of young librarians from the state library school. There are growing branch library activities and a mobile library calls regularly at all the city schools. The central library also houses the rural library headquarters for the Indre-et-Loire area. Expenditure on library services is liberal, about two percent of the city budget. The results achieved are heartening, with circulating figures averaging 4·6 issues per inhabitant per annum.

Troyes (70,000) has a collection of no less than 90,000 rare books. New premises have added forty percent to the working area of the library services. There is now a large children's library, a ' story hour ' room and space for exhibitions and other functions.

Improvements to library services are not, however, limited to the group of fifty ' classified ' municipal libraries. The other municipal libraries have, in many cases, recognised the pressing need for higher standards in the facilities provided. A few of the local initiatives taken over the last few years are quoted below.

La Roche-sur-Yon (25,000) has acquired a new library with a high standard in furnishings and other arrangements. It has greatly increased its book circulation figures: books issued in March 1969 totalling 6,482, as opposed to 1,898 in the same period the previous year. It has some 8,000 volumes on open access. The lending library (200 square metres) is larger than the ' *salle de travail* ' which measures 170 square metres and has seats for seventy two readers. There is a *discothèque,* an exhibition area, and a commodious book stack.

Riom (15,500) in Puy-de-Dôme inaugurated large adapted premises in 1968. The new location offers a much larger library, an exhibition hall, a children's corner, and two rooms for meetings.

Beauvais (36,000) opened its third branch recently. This is in a new development zone and provides 100 square metres of additional library space.

Fontaine (20,000) near Grenoble, has recently inaugurated a most attractive L-shaped building overlooking a public garden. As in the case of the new premises at Le Havre, a large glazed area faces the street.

Saint-Martin-d'Hères (20,000) is another municipality near to Grenoble. Its new library adjoins a school medical centre. Well planned and attractively furnished, it is designed to accommodate an eventual stock of 50,000 volumes.

Colomiers (12,000) near Toulouse, has initiated a lending library and reading room which is open daily from 17.00 to 20.00 (Sundays and Mondays excepted). Contact with the regional *bibliothèque centrale de prêt* is good and to add to existing stocks the municipality raised F5,000 for new books. In addition a long loan of 2,000 books was made from BCP stocks.

In the Paris suburban area, noteworthy library work is being carried out in the highly populated areas of *Sarcelles, Levallois-Perret* and *Massy.* In *Sarcelles,* rapid expansion took place and large housing developments increased the population very rapidly; the existing small town was ' *Sarcellée* ', to use the term now applied to new high-density areas. There were no local amenities but a few enthusiasts started a library in 1958. This has now developed into a flourishing service with a full programme of extension activities.

Massy, another dormitory town, has a new library which is under the special care of the national library school and which is used as a training library for library students. It is also the natural site for any trials of new methods.

Other recent useful initiatives have been reported from, to name a few authorities, Bagnolet, Chartes, Douai and Barentin.

Some statistical analyses have indicated the size of the problem which currently faces the *Direction* and the local authorities. One such report suggests that out of 606 municipalities 145, or 23·92 percent have no municipal library whatsoever. The count was made in the *Enquête statistique sur les bibliothèques municipales* of the *Commission des Communes Urbaines* of the *Association des Maires de France*. The report is undated but the figures appear to refer to 1965, since which date there have been some improvements. The statistics should, therefore, be treated with caution. The figures refer to a sample of 461 municipalities, but the replies to the various questions were incomplete.

Book stocks (totals)	Libraries	percent
up to 5,000	101	21·91
5,000-10,000	85	18·44
10,000-50,000	157	34·05
over 50,000	116	25·16
No response	2	·44
Lending stocks		
up to 500	5	1·08
500-2,000	24	5·20
2,000-10,000	185	40·14
10,000-30,000	132	28·64
30,000-60,000	43	9·33
60,000-100,000	15	3·25
over 100,000	16	3·47
No response	41	8·89

Books bought (1965)	percent	Libraries
up to 100	74	16·12
100-300	120	25·94
300-700	104	22·45
700-1,000	46	10·02
1,000-2,000	52	11·32
over 2,000	46	10·02
No response	19	4·13
Periodicals received (1965)		
none	72	15·62
up to 10	107	23·22
10-20	58	12·58
20-50	75	16·27
50 to 100	50	10·84
over 100	59	12·80
No response	40	8·67
Days open per week. Lending services		
5-6 days	189	50·00
4 days	42	9·11
1-3 days	223	48·38
Under one day	2	0·43
No response	5	1·08
Municipalities with branch libraries		
With branches (*annexes*)	75	16·26
Without branches	287	62·26
No response	99	21·48
Membership formalities		
No formalities	92	14·4
Six months' residence	68	10·6
Identity card only	243	37·9
Other	238	37·1
Membership and/or loan fees		
No charge at all	80	17·35
Membership fee only	111	24·08
Free membership but charge per loan	133	28·86
Membership fee *and* charge per loan	111	24·08
No response	26	5·63

Open access	Libraries	percent
None	63	13·66
In reading room only	34	7·37
In home lending only	110	23·87
Throughout library	248	53·80
No response	6	1·30

Personnel		
1 staff member	314	66·11
2 staff members	80	17·35
3-4	43	9·32
5-7	13	2·81
8-10	2	0·43
11 and over	5	1·08
No response	4	0·86

Qualifications of staff		
No qualified staff	256	55·54
Some qualified staff	53	11·49
All qualified	77	16·70
No response	75	16·26

Municipal budgets for libraries (1965)		
up to 1,000F	41	8·89
1,000-2,000F	49	10·62
2,000-5,000F	92	19·96
5,000-10,000F	87	18·88
10,000-30,000F	104	22·56
30,000-50,000F	29	6·30
50,000-70,000F	17	3·68
over 70,000F	19	4·12
No response	23	4·98

A more recent survey has been made and reported in the *Bulletin d'informations of the Association des Bibliothécaires Français* (no 65, *4th quarter*, 1969). This concerns the densely populated Paris suburban areas which contain heavy concentrations of low priced housing developments, blocks of luxury apartments, private houses, factories and offices. It is suggested that twenty one out of a total of 114 local authorities lacked a public library. The twenty one *communes* concerned had a total population of 119,000 inhabitants. Some of these authorities may, however, have lending facilities from *bibliothèques centrales de prêt*. Where libraries are provided, 73 percent are said to share space in schools and other public buildings. Although many of the local authorities are extensive the development of neighbourhood libraries has been slow. Of a sample of 118 libraries:

16 (13·6 percent) had one branch
10 (8·5 percent) had two branches
1 only had three branches

Mobile libraries are a possible preliminary step. However only 9·6 percent of the local authorities had made such provision. Most of the buildings were old, although two thirds of the sample had benefited from renovations since 1950. Most libraries were cramped. The largest libraries in the sample were:

Mantes-la-Jolie	1,330 square metres
Melun	806
Vincennes	750
St Maur les Fosses	670
Boulogne	592
Clamart	567
St Ouen	558

Only seven of the 118 *communes* provide one book per head of population. With 2·7 books per inhabitant, Coulommiers was the best provided for; at the lower end of the scale fifty two municipalities (44 percent) possessed between ·25 and ·50 books per head. Twenty two institutions (18·7 percent) had only one book for every four inhabitants. Few libraries in this group had profited from the Revolutionary confiscations, the exception being Saint-Denis. This has 77,000 books in its reference collection, compared with 53,000 in the lending service. In broad terms, however, 94·2 percent of the libraries are unable to offer a book per head. Among those in the ·25 books per head category will be found the names of seven fairly large communities of 48,000 to 90,000 people.

The general picture of facilities within the libraries emerges from the following table:

Facilities:	Total in sample 118	percent 100
Reading room in addition to lending library	56	47
Children's library	37	31
Gramophone records	24	20
Separate office for librarian	47	40
Reserve book stack	45	38
Staff work room	36	31
Staff room	29	25
Lecture hall	12	10
Utility room for films etc	35	30
Open access	100	84·8
Special furniture in children's library	45	37
Telephone, central libraries	68	57·6
Telephone, branch libraries	16	14
Duplicator	18	15

The French government is deeply concerned with the problem of ' cultural deserts ' in the densely settled areas, not only in the Paris region, but also in the large housing and industrial development schemes in all of the major cities.

The part which the community library could play is obvious to all, although the size of the programme required is daunting. However, within the limits of its budget, the *Direction* has set in motion a programme of some magnitude. It includes the construction of new central and branch libraries and the reorganisation and extension of existing premises. Large quantities of new furniture and other equipment are involved. Details of the programmes for 1968, 1969 and 1970 follow, together with details of the building standards suggested.

PUBLIC LIBRARIES
Direction des bibliothèques et de la lecture publique
Programme financed in 1968:

Construction of new buildings
Central libraries:

Bron	1,600 square metres	
Caen	5,000	
Creil	1,800	
Longwy	1,510	
Saint-Mandé	900	
Saint-Nazaire	3,510	
Tarbes	2,700	

Branch libraries:

Bourges	1,250	Quartier des Gibjoncs
Brest	500	Bouguen
Mulhouse	710	Quartier des Coteaux
Perpignan	215	Annexe du Moulin à Vent
Rouen	500	Annexe des Sapins
Saint-Dié	700	Annexe Kellermann
Toulouse	360	Annexe de Bellefontaine (ZUP du Mirail)

Extensions

Les Sables d'Olonne	1,000	an extension to a cultural centre to accommodate the library.
Levallois-Perret	300	
Limoges (1)	1,500	
Limoges (2)	680	
Pau	1,600	

Reorganisations and transfers

Bourge-la-reine	650
Le Mans	490
Mont-de-Marsan	670
Saint-Etienne	800
Saint-Malo	950
Sarcelles	640
Vincennes	760

Branch libraries:

Poitiers	720
Rouen	200

Programme financed in 1969

Construction of new buildings
Central library
    Malakoff   1,700   square metres
Branch library
    Annecy   112   Annexe de la cité Novel

Extensions
    Mamers   160   reorganisation and extension of the central library

    Soissons   1,490   reorganisation:
                                              650 square metres
                                 extension:
                                                840 square metres

Reorganisations and transfers
    Autun   280
    Auxerre   435
    Avallon   285
    Joigny   280
    Lezignan   230
    Millau   800
    Rodez   850
    Tourcoing   480
Branch library for children
    Louviers   350

Programme financed in 1970

Construction of new buildings
Central libraries
    Neuilly-Plaisance   800
    Pantin   1,600
Branch library
    Chambery   350   Annexe du quartier Maché

Extensions
Central libraries
    Cambrai   1,370   square metres
    Chateaudun   760

Reorganisations and transfers
Central libraries
    Chatellerault   220   establishment of a children's library and book store in a house adjoining the library
    Redon   290
Branch libraries
    Aix-en-Provence   240
    Besançon   200

Building standards of the *Direction des Bibliothèques et de la Lecture Publique*

The following programmes apply to municipalities in which there are no stocks of rare books. If these exist, then additional allowance must be made, especially in the stacks.

Municipal library for a town of 5,000-6,000
Public service areas
    Adult reading-room/lending library
10 seats: 6 to 7,000 books on open access   130   square metres
    Children's library
    30 seats: 1,500 to 2,000 books on open access   80

Services   210
    Administration   30
    Office   20
    Store   20
                                      70
                                    280
Circulation, heating, cloaks and toilets for
    public and staff (about 25 per cent)   70
                                      350

Municipal library, town of 6,000 to 10,000
Public service areas
    Adult reading room/lending library

14-18 seats; 7 to 10,000 books		160 square metres
Children's library		
40 seats; 2-4,000 books	120	
Multi-purpose room	40	
		320
Service		
Administration	30	
Office	20	
Store	30	
		80
Circulation, heating, cloaks etc		100
		500

Town or urban grouping with 10,000- 20,000 inhabitants
Public service areas
    Adult reading room/lending library

20-30 seats; 10,000-16,000 vols		240 square metres
Children's library		
40-45 seats; 4,000-6,000 vols	140	
Discothèque corner	20	
Multi-purpose room (meetings, exhibitions etc)	50	
		450
Services		
Administration	30	
Librarian and secretary	20	
Office	20	
Book store	40	
		110
Add 25 percent for heating, cloaks etc		140
		700

Town or urban grouping with 20,000- 30,000 inhabitants
Public service areas
    Adult lending library

14,000-18,000 vols open access	330	square metres
Reading/reference		
30-35 seats; 6-8,000 vols	160	
Children		
40-50 seats; 4,000-6,000 volumes	150	
Multi-purpose room	70	
Discothèque	40	
	———	
		750
Services		
Administration	50	
Offices, librarian and secretary	20	
Offices 3/4 staff	40	
	———	
		110
Stacks		
For about 10,000 books		60
Circulation, heating, cloaks etc		280
		———
		1,200

Municipal library, 30,000 - 45,000 inhabitants
Public service areas
    Adult lending;

14/18,000 vols on open access	330	square metres
Reference/reading room;		
35/45 seats; 7/9,000 vols	180	
Children's library;		
40/45 seats; 4/6,000 vols	150	
Discothèque	50	
Multi-purpose room	80	
	———	
		790

52

Services
Administration and book preparation	90 square metres
Librarian and secretary	20
Offices 4/5 staff	45
Workshop	35
Garage for urban bookmobile	60
Caretaker's flat	60
	310

Stacks
For about 20,000 volumes	120
Circulation, heating, cloaks etc	380
	1,600

Municipal branch library for 15,000 inhabitants
Public services areas
Reading and lending (books and gramophone records) adults 10 seats; 8/12,000 vols	180 square metres
Children's library	
40 seats; 4/6,000 vols	140
Multi-purpose room	40
	360

Services
Administration	20
Office	20
	40
Circulation, heating, cloaks etc	100
	500

FURTHER READING
Baudin, G: 'Enquêtes sur les bibliothèques dans la Région Parisienne, 1968-9'. ABF *Bulletin d'Informations*, 66-67, 1970.

Cahiers des bibliothèques de France. II Lecture publique rurale et urbaine. Direction des Bibliothèques et de la Lecture Publique, 1956.

Répertoire des bibliothèques de France. II Bibliothèques de province. Direction des Bibliothèques et de la Lecture Publique, 1951.

Bulletin d'informations (Q). Association des Bibliothécaires Français, 1948-.

Lectures et bibliothèques (Q). Association des Bibliothèques Français. *Section des Bibliothèques Publiques.*

Hassenforder, J: ' Development of public libraries in France, the United Kingdom and the United States '. *Unesco Bulletin for libraries,* XXII (1) 1968.

Hassenforder, J: *Développement comparé des bibliothèques publiques en France, en Grande Bretagne et aux Etats-Unis dans la seconde moité du XIXe siécle* (1850-1914). Paris, Cercle de la libraire, 1967.

Neveux, P and Dacier, E: *Les richesses des bibliothèques provinciales de France.* Paris, two volumes 1932.

CHAPTER SIX

Non municipal general libraries

In addition to the local authority general libraries mentioned so far, account must be taken of various private organisations which have concerned themselves with library provision. These institutions have attempted to provide a service either because it was felt that the local authorities had failed to meet the needs, or because the facilities offered were insufficiently attractive.

The best known of these initiatives are the *bibliothèques pour tous* (libraries for all). The *Service Culture et Bibliothèques pour Tous* was founded in 1934 by the *Action Catholique Générale Féminine,* and its shop windows are a familiar sight in many French towns. It is the largest network in the private sector. In 1969 it had 1,800 libraries and 1,200 deposit stations. Its aim is to provide the family unit with reading materials which achieve a required standard in content and presentation.

In order to be sure of reaching the man in the street, emphasis has been placed on separating the libraries from ecclesiastical buildings. Wherever possible the libraries are in shopping districts with shop window facilities. In 1956 there were 257 such shop branches. This number had grown to 650 by 1959. A wide range of readers is attracted, not all of whom are active church members. The book collections are bright and attractive, and there is free access to the shelves. Certain books in stock are restricted to responsible readers.

Family subscriptions are levied and a charge is made for each loan. The libraries are organised on a *département* basis, there being ninety two regional offices and a head office in Paris. Here a team of some fifteen trained librarians provides technical help and compiles booklists. Each library remits twenty five per cent of its income to the departmental office to provide a regional reserve of books. Circulating collections are sent out to strengthen the book stocks of the individual libraries.

Thought has been given to the need for professional training. There is close liaison with the library school of the *Institut Catholique* in Paris which provided the original trained staff. A correspondence course was started in 1941 to train those responsible for the lending libraries. For those concerned with children's libraries a course, based on child psychology, was added in 1963. Conferences on departmental, regional, and national levels help to train personnel. By 1969, 5,955 students had gained diplomas. Several have taken the state diploma known as CAFB. The monthly periodical *Les notes bibliographiques* discusses practical problems and keeps staff in touch with new developments, and also provides an excellent book selection guide. Each entry is fully catalogued and classified (Dewey). There is a careful annotation. In some entries the reader's attention is directed towards other books which deal with the same or related themes. There is a separate guide to children's books, *Livres jeunes aujourd'hui,* a monthly journal which started in 1970, where recommendations are made by experienced panels. Good writing, illustration and presentation are encouraged. Circulation figures and membership totals are compiled methodically, some recent returns being:

Year	Total circulation	Children's books issued
1956/7	5,772,478	808,914
1962/3	7,299,187	2,238,193
1965/6	7,924,852	2,620,095
1967/8	8,633,300	3,012,198

There are eleven *discothèque* libraries, and in 1967/8 11,543 gramophone records were issued, most loans being made of classical music. A useful service is provided in summer holiday resorts and summer camps. At a time when school libraries and most public libraries are closed, the *bibliothèques pour tous* provide reading materials in the vacation centres. In 1969 the service provided 835 such holiday libraries. As far as rural coverage is concerned, there is a tendency to discontinue the less well used deposit stations. There were 2,976 of these in 1956, but the number had dropped to 1,200 by 1969.

The *Centre Laïque de Lecture Publique* is a section of the *Ligue Française de l' Enseignment*. This organisation seeks to establish and to maintain a chain of *bibliothèques circulantes*. There are over 4,000 of these, mostly in community centres, holiday centres, youth clubs and student hostels. The *Centre Laïque* is interested in encouraging organisations to build up their own libraries. It will therefore lend or sell boxes of books on various themes. The boxes contain thirty to thirty five books and a charge of F12 per month is made for each box. It also has a centralised book buying service which secures a discount for the participating library.

The *Centre* publishes a review of books, *Lectures culturelles*, in which about ninety books are analysed in each issue. Special issues for children's books are published twice a year. Advice is given on the administration of libraries, as well as scripts which are provided for talks on various books and on different subjects of interest to community centre members.

WORKS LIBRARIES

Works councils are set up by all companies with fifty or more people on the payroll. There are about 25,000 such *comités d'enterprise* and they represent several million workers. A subvention is paid by the employers. This amounted to F780 millions in 1967. Of this total, twenty percent is directed towards cultural activities. Works libraries receive a share which amounts to an estimated ten million francs annually.

There had been a few works libraries in northern and other industrial zones in the nineteenth century, but development did not take place until the legislation which established works councils. Naturally enough, conditions vary widely from plant to plant. In many cases the library lacks a special room and is left in the care of the welfare officer. At the other end of the scale, however, one must note the remarkable library of the Renault factory in Billancourt, near Paris. This receives an annual grant of almost F300,000, or F9·3 per head of the labour force, and has a staff of eleven. The bookstock was over 60,000 volumes and the annual circulation stood at 108,560 in 1967. It adds 3,000 books each year. There is a central library, but seventy five percent of the books are issued in the lunch break from two vehicles which tour the extensive site. Classification is by UDC. Immigrant workers from North Africa, Spain and Portugal are specially provided with books in their own languages. There is a separate 4,000 book library for the 450 students in the school for apprentices.

The railways of the French system, SNCF, probably constitute the largest single unit in this category. There are 372 railway libraries distributed among the six railway regions, with each regional group having its own budget. Book loans totalled 3·7 millions in 1967. Over a million books are placed at the disposal of 320,000 railwaymen and their families. Retired staff members also benefit. The south-east region makes use of a celebrated ' bibliofer ', a railway coach converted into a mobile library.

Motor manufacturers are well represented among the better supported libraries and the Paris head office of BP reports a record membership of forty five per cent of the effective strength. Some examples of use and financial support are below:

	Payroll	Library grant per head	Library members (percentage of payroll)	Books lent per annum per head
SNECMA	3,700	F2·5	8	3·8
BP (Paris)	1,150	F4	45	9
Berliet	12,000	F7	12	0·1
Renault (Flins)	10,000	F0·8	ʔ0	2

It seems likely that the impetus to develop works libraries originated in the weakness of the smaller public libraries. Many of these have, as has been indicated, a very small staff. Lunch hour closing is normal and few keep open long enough in the evenings to provide a service for commuters. It is possible also, that the industrial and other workers see the public institution as the preserve of the scholarly man and are wary of using it. In

Annecy, in 1957, as many people used the libraries of the factories as read in the municipal library, according to a local census.

There are acknowledged weaknesses, however, in the works libraries. A Unesco study in 1961 suggested that only six percent of them had trained librarians. The whole question of independent industrial libraries is of interest to the French library profession. In a full discussion of the situation (' Les bibliothèques sur les lieux de travail '. *Bulletin des bibliothèques de France,* March 1962) M Julien Cain said that works libraries were neither the only nor the best solution. The future lay in the development of public libraries and rural library services open to all, irrespective of occupation.

HOSPITAL LIBRARIES

The public assistance hospitals of Paris have a library service with a headquarters organisation which places book orders, carries out the technical preparation and allocates books to hospitals and sanatoria. The stock is classified by Dewey. The allocation varies between five and six books per bed in surgical wards, to twelve or so in sanatoria.

Where possible there are special library rooms, but in older hospitals cupboards are used to store books. Patients confined to bed are visited by staff wheeling book trolleys—' *chariots de consolation* ' as Georges Duhamel called them. The service is free and there is no limit to the number of loans. The newer libraries have space for book exhibitions and group meetings of readers.

The service was started in a difficult financial period and remains understaffed, though volunteer assistants help out. Loans include about sixty percent fiction and 650,000 were made in 1958. Libraries in sanatoria can be fairly large units and are sustained by an addition to the daily rate charged for the patient. There are, in addition to books, collections of gramophone records from which recitals are arranged. Special facilities and books are provided for immigrant patients.

University students receive a special service if they fall ill while following a course. They have their own medical service, the *Fondation Santé des Etudiants de France.* Library facilities are provided by BUCEM, the *Bibliothèque Universitaire Centrale des Etudiants Malades*. This has new premises in 12 rue Boileau, Paris 16. Part of the 28,000 bookstock is stored in ' Compactus ' rolling shelves. Purchase and preparation is centralised, and catalogue cards are sent to the nineteen hospitals in the group. The students have a very large sanatorium near Grenoble. BUCEM was organised in 1953, and is now part of the ensemble of libraries of Paris university which is under the control of the *Direction*.

ARMY LIBRARIES

The *Ministère des Armées* has a social obligation to provide reading materials for its regular establishment and also for the young men called up each year for national service. Libraries are, therefore, available in about 700 regimental centres and in some fifty military hospitals. There are a further fifty, or so, in army industrial establishments. Isolated units may make use of *bibliothèques circulantes,* or boxes containing a selection of twenty five books fed from a central pool which receives about 50,000 new books annually.

LIBRARIES FOR THE BLIND

A general collection is provided for blind readers at the *Bibliothèque Braille* by the Union des Aveugles de Guerre which circulates 15,000 book titles. In addition its *Livre parlé* service, which dates from 1943, has about 72,000 recordings in disc or tape form.

FURTHER READING

Cacérès, G and others: *La lecture.* Paris, Editions du Seuil, 1961.

Charpentreau, J and others: *Le livre et la lecture en France.* Paris, Les Editions Ouvrières, 1968.

CHAPTER SEVEN

Children's libraries and school libraries

France is a young country in the sense that fully one third of the population is under twenty years of age. It has a lively literature for the young, which extends from the fairy tales of Charles Perrault to the present day heroes, among whom one could number ' Tintin ' and 'Asterix the Gaul '. However it has its quota of *bandes desinées,* or comics, and the average eight year old will consume between two and four of these a week. A 1959 survey by the *Syndicat Nationale des Editeurs,* the publishers' association suggests that among the seven to fifteen year olds:

   9 percent do not read at all

   32 percent read about nine books per year

   38 percent read about fifteen books per year

   21 percent read more than twenty five books per year.

Exclusive of school texts some forty million children's books were produced in 1963. Sales accounted for about seven percent of total book sales. Although an early start had been made with school libraries, in 1862, work with children in the public library sense of the term made its appearance only in 1924. At that date the book committee of the Children's Library of New York opened the library known as *L'Heure Joyeuse* in rue Boutebrie in the Latin Quarter of Paris. It was a pilot project with a stock of 11,000 books on open access and classified by the Dewey scheme. The city of Paris took over the original children's library in the rue Boutebrie in 1925 and has since provided *bibliothèques enfantines* in many of its neighbourhood branches.

The librarian of *L'Heure Joyeuse, Mlle* Gruny, became a pioneer in this field and many librarians were trained in library work with children. In spite of overcrowded and generally inadequate premises, many other municipal libraries made space for children's corners.

New buildings opened subsequently have included properly planned and equipped libraries. Lille municipal library, for example, has a large and attractive children's library with its own separate entrance. There are over 4,000 volumes in the lending department, a special corner for the very young, and well-chosen reference books for the older users. An internal stairway leads to a section in which drawing, painting and other activities are carried out under the guidance of a trained and sympathetic staff. The children produce their own magazine, *Entre nous*. Story hours are arranged and an attractive, secluded garden is used for outdoor activities in fine weather. In addition, books for the young are available in the city branch libraries.

In the same way, one may find excellent and varied programmes to encourage reading in many of the larger and better-housed city libraries. Tours, Caen, Bordeaux and Toulouse could be quoted in this connection.

There is a uniformly warm response on the part of the children. This may, possibly, be a natural reaction to the somewhat rigid and high pressure programmes of formal instruction in the primary and secondary schools. Library authorities in both the public and the private sectors agree that where attractive facilities exist the younger readers make immediate and extended use of them. The same reaction is to be observed where only a book service is available, as in the case of the urban and rural mobile library services.

Private enterprise remains a feature of the developmental work in this field. The association *La Joie par les Livres* financed, built and opened in 1965 a children's library of advanced design in Clamart. This is a suburb of Paris in which 10,000 people live, many in large housing estates. The municipality gave the site and takes care of maintenance costs, and will eventually be responsible for the entire project. There are three trained librarians, table accommodation for eighty readers and space for 10,000 to 12,000 books.

La Joie par les Livres was founded in 1963 to encourage the development of children's libraries. In association with the French library association it publishes *La bulletin d'analyses de livres*. This is a quarterly publication which provides a book selection service and reviews books. We have already noted, in a previous reference, the reviewing journal of children's books entitled *Livres jeunes aujourd'hui*.

Various awards are made annually to encourage the production of good children's books. These include:

Prix ' Jean Macé '. *Ligue française de l'enseignment;*
Prix de la ' *Joie par les livres* ';
Grand Prix de la Litérature Enfantine du Salon de l'Enfance.

Opening hours in local authority and other children's libraries are generally limited. In some cases books are available only on Thursdays, when the schools close, or on Saturday afternoons. The hours at Clamart are:

Tuesdays, Wednesdays, Fridays   16.00-19.00
Thursdays   10.00-19.00
Saturdays   12.00-19.00

In Toulouse and some other large libraries the readers are divided into groups for which separate arrangements are made. The Toulouse division is:

enfants: 6-15 years
jeunes: 15-18 years

The link with adolescent readers is often helped if the library services the various youth clubs.

French libraries arrange an impressive number of children's library activities and in these the readers themselves often play a full part. One library (Tours) reports the following year's work:

3	puppet shows	230	spectators
11	slide projection shows	235	,,
62	story hours	2,038	listeners
27	record recitals	520	,,
24	book talks	1,010	,,
395	films shown	9,090	spectators

5	model club functions	60	participants
111	meetings TV club	5,518	,,
81	meetings of an art group	4,093	,,
278	class visits		
41	meetings of smaller groups		
29	meetings of a choral group		
5	exhibitions		
1	recital by the choir	120	audience
52	sessions on the use of the library for school classes		

This programme was carried out in the library and also in the premises of a nearby *maison de jeunes* or youth club.

The building standards of the *Direction* recommend that new buildings or adapted premises should make adequate provision for young readers. For details see the appendix to chapter six.

In addition to the individual authorities named so far, good facilities will be found in: Angoulême, Bagnolet, Beauvais, Brest, Chartres, Douai, Grenoble, Le Havre, Lorient, Lyon, Mulhouse, Nice, Rouen, St-Dié, Troyes and many other centres.

School libraries date from 1860 when a circular required each schoolmaster to maintain one. A later regulation of 1915 laid down that each primary school should have a library supported by grants from the state and from local authorities. If possible there should be a special room. It should be open not only to scholars but also to former pupils, parents and others. However maintenance was faulty and only about 43,000 such libraries were still in existence in 1947 with a total of 8½ million volumes. Various writers have suggested that the collections were in a poor state and that only half of them were really effective. Under a *décret*, no 65-335 of April 1965, wider powers were given to the councils of the departments whereby school libraries could be financed. A recent enquiry into the situation was reported in *La voix de l'edition*, no 77 March/April 1967. Replies came from 6,398 schools of which forty percent were urban and sixty percent were in rural settings. It would appear that the lack of funds which afflicted the 1860 scheme persists. Expenditure on school libraries per head per annum was:

Fo.10 or less 11 percent of the sample
0.20   19
0.30   13
0.40   37
0.50   10
0.80   7
F1.00 or over   3

To secure funds school authorities had to appeal to many sources. The municipal subventions accounted for only 29·36 percent of the total. Additional money is raised by means of membership fees, fines and profits from various social events.

Libraries, the report indicates, exist in eighty percent of the schools. For the most part these are class libraries, although 11·8 percent of the sample reported having a centralised school library. Such school libraries have a better chance of evolving in the new groups of schools which are being developed as the smaller rural schools close down. The collections are limited in size. Half of the sample had less than 150 books. In general terms it was suggested that the number of books per child was 0·41 compared with eleven in Sweden and six to ten in the UK and the USA.

However the *Direction's* policy in regard to mobile libraries carrying children's books is, it seems, beginning to bear results. Of the sample 11% of the schools were in receipt of mobil library services which could be in addition to such book resources as were already provided.

The library services to rural areas of the *bibliothèques centrales de prêt* are extremely well used by schoolchildren. The 1968 report on *La Lecture Publique* suggests that between fifty and seventy five percent of children in the areas served were registered readers. In its purchases of books the *Direction* spends one third of the fund on children's books.

In the field of secondary education the development of ' central ' as opposed to class libraries dates from about 1969, and owed much to the work of *Mme Brunchwig*, the Inspectrice Générale concerned with libraries. However, progress has been slow, according to a report *Les bibliothèques dans l'enseignment du second degré* published in 1969. Only about fifteen percent of

65

3

the *lycées* had such provision. These 200 or so institutions were examined. It appeared that the average library consisted of 3,463 books or 2·6 per pupil served. Only one fifth of the sample had an adjoining room for group work. Most libraries were in one room, averaging 72·4 square metres, and capable of providing thirty three reading room places. This would seat about 2·5 percent of the total enrolment.

Mixed and girls schools were more likely to have a library than boys schools. The figures were:

mixed:	45·2	percent
girls:	37	percent
boys:	17·8	percent

Bookstocks totalled 750,000 in 1966, fiction making up less than half of the total. The average library takes ten or eleven periodicals. About 19·3 percent provide gramophone record libraries.

Financial support comes mainly from the state:

ministry credits:	40 percent
additional credits:	16·6
membership fees:	25·5
gifts:	4·6
other sources:	13·3

In addition the Ministry of Education sends books directly; each library receives an average 267 books annually. However, there are some suggestions that these cause unwanted duplications.

Lycée librarians were well equipped as to general education. 71·3 percent were graduates and 12·4 percent had some *licence* certificates following the *baccalaureat*. Of the graduates, 42·5 percent had read modern languages. On the other hand 84·2 percent had taken no professional library training. Of the trained librarians, sixty percent had obtained the CAFB.

Open access is general, and seventy one percent of the sample use the Dewey decimal classification. Home lending is permitted by 96·3 percent. Some libraries offer useful documentation services; about half organise exhibitions. However there is no equality of status with teaching staff.

Each academic district has a regional centre for educational documentation (*Centre Regional de Documentation Pédagogique*). Among their other functions the CRDP units provide teachers in training with materials required in connection with their practical and theoretical work. Many of the new centres are in new buildings with good equipment. Their libraries replaced the former *bibliothèques académiques de prêt*.

For teachers in schools ' general libraries ' were provided following a ministerial order of 1838. The intention was to ensure a stock of books to be used in connection with teaching activities, and also to help teachers to prepare for higher qualifications. Such libraries are assisted by the Ministry of Education and the *Institut Pédagogique National*. However, the multiplication of many small units resulted in a less than satisfactory service in some areas. A circular issued by the Ministry of Education in 1951 strongly urged the amalgamation of these small libraries into larger collections which might serve the needs of an entire town. This had been done in Marseille, where a '*Foyer Universitaire*' had been set up. Another cooperative venture of this type is the local centres for educational documentation which were established at the Lycée Jeanson-de-Sailly and elsewhere. In 1967 there were approximately 600 of these in service. It is currently suggested that these centres and the *lycée* libraries for pupils should join forces to become a *Service de Documentation et d'Information Pédagogique* in each establishment.

FURTHER READING

Bouyssi, M: ' Les sections pour la jeunesse dans les bibliothèques de province. *Bulletin des bibliothèques de France*, July 1964.

Dubois, R: ' Connaître les réactions des jeunes lecteurs ' and Soriano, H: ' La naissance du livre pour enfants.' *Bulletin des bibliothèques de France*, November 1966.

Institut Pédagogique National: *La lecture chez les jeunes et les bibliothèques dans l'enseignment du second degré.* 1969.

Institut Pédagogique National : *Le service de documentation et d'information pédagogique des établissements du second degré.* 1968.

Juhel : ' La bibliothèque dans les etablissements du second degré '. *L'education nationale,* December 1950.

CHAPTER EIGHT

Rural libraries

LA BIBLIOTHÈQUE CENTRALE DE PRET: The rural population has been in decline for a century. At one time seventy five percent of the total population lived in the country. The present level is thirty-eight percent and there are signs that changes in agricultural methods will reduce still further the rural proportion. The small communities, naturally, find it difficult to make adequate library provision.

Certain experiments had been made in the Aisne region and elsewhere after the 1914-18 war whereby collections were sent to villages and exchanged. A similar service started in Seine-Inférieure in 1921. In the 1940's a small mobile library served communities in the Dordogne.

After the liberation the *Direction des Bibliothèques* was created and this was followed by the decision to organise *bibliothèques centrales de prêt* to serve the extensive country districts. There are currently forty nine of these and three in other French communities Guadeloupe, Martinique and La Réunion. They are financed by the state, though local subventions may meet approximately twenty to thirty percent of the costs. In addition some have an income from membership fees. The chief officers are fully trained members of the state *corps* of librarians. The 1966 state budget was about $4\frac{1}{2}$ million francs. In addition, state grants are paid to certain *associations départmental de lecture publique*.

In 1946, eight units were created, and nine in the following year. However the progress has not been even. With about half of the areas yet to be provided with a service, the *Direction* currently adds between four and five libraries each year.

The *département* concerned must agree to provide a temporary home for the library and to contribute towards running expenses; the annual sum varies between F5,000 and F30,000. In addition, it must provide a free site of about 3,000 square metres for the new headquarters building.

An analytical survey published in the *Bulletin des bibliothèques de France*, July 1967 put forward the following estimates of costs:

average cost to the state of a BCP F109,612 per annum
cost per inhabitant (14 million
   theoretically served)   Fo.31   ,,
local subventions per inhabitant Fo.10   ,,
total cost of BCP per inhabitant   Fo.41   ,,

Local interest is maintained through a consultative committee which includes representatives of the council of the department, local mayors, the university and voluntary librarians.

The central library is normally in the chief town, although there are some exceptions. The initial staff establishment was meagre; one librarian, one sublibrarian, one typist, one driver, one mobile library or delivery van. This meant that books had to be made available through deposit stations which had unpaid volunteer librarians. Management rules were drawn up in 1955. The Dewey classification system was adopted, and duplicated catalogues and special subject lists were prepared.

The service often operated from a corner of an existing library which was itself overcrowded. That of the Rhône area sheltered in a wing of the Lyon municipal library from 1947 to 1963. It had three ornate rooms with exquisite wood carvings. An ornamental staircase, ' glacial in winter ', made the movement of boxes difficult. Books stood two layers deep on shelves which extended upwards for four metres.

In 1964 a site of 1,500 square metres was ceded and the first specially designed library was built. This is on two levels; on the upper level mobile libraries back into loading bays, there being a large stack and work space for twelve people; and on the lower floor there is a gramophone record library, duplicating room, meeting room, canteen and box store.

A more recent example of the shared building will be seen in Strasbourg. Here the Bas-Rhin library occupies part of the Science and Technical library of the *Bibliothèque Nationale et Universi-*

taire. However, the fact that such a library cannot ever be extended has caused the *Direction* to reject the solution. In future new buildings will be built on open sites which permit extensions. From 1967 to 1968 no fewer than five new buildings were provided at Montpellier, Rodez, Besançon, Orléans and Rouen. These are devised to provide approximately 650 square metres of floor space. Such smaller buildings, costing less than F500,000 need not be particularised in the French state budget and this makes for flexibility in the programme. The restricted superficial area does not permit the customary flat for the caretaker. Planning is extremely interesting and practical. See the article 'Bibliothèques centrales de prêt by Roland Descaves (*Bulletin des bibliothèques de France*, July 1969) for a full discussion.

The evolution of methods can be traced in the *Cahiers des bibliothèques de France, Direction des Bibliothêques,* second volume, 1954.

The original restriction to one mobile library meant a very full programme of deliveries. There followed a period when collections made up at HQ could be added to by local librarians who chose books directly from the shelves. The third stage was to offer direct choice from the shelves of the vehicle. This method also made direct access to the shelves possible for schoolchildren and other readers. The frequency of visits depended on circumstances. Deposit stations were most often in schools but could equally be in the town hall, a municipal library or in a community centre. A 1961-66 analysis revealed the following pattern:

Area	School	Mairie	Municipal Library	Other
Aisne	637	51	17	42
Isère	570	15	—	55
Pas-de-Calais	968	9	3	47

However, the deposit system was found to be most unsatisfactory. The local librarian was unpaid and it was difficult to find enthusiasts. When schools closed it was often impossible to find an alternative location for the books. Membership and circulation statistics remained incomplete since only a minority of the *dépositaires* made returns.

A vigorous attempt has, therefore, been made to increase the number of mobile libraries, many of which now offer direct lending services. Six areas have been selected in which the fleets of mobile libraries have been increased substantially. These are, Cantal, Doubs, Eure, Rhin-Bas, Pas-de-Calais and Seine-et-Marne. At the time of writing Pas-de-Calais has twelve vehicles and a book stock of 260,000 volumes. It is estimated that each mobile library can serve up to 3,000 readers. The number of deposit stations is falling as mobile services increase. The service to schools continues, in the Pas-de-Calais, throughout July and a double ration of books is issued to carry readers through August. A mobile library based on Boulogne carries on through August, allowing coastal holidaymakers to become members with minimum formalities. It is hoped to develop fixed branch libraries in this region. Where books are deposited in municipal libraries, a trained member of staff can be attached for a considerable period to put the municipal collection in order.

The areas yet to receive a BCP have a population of about fourteen million. Standards in the existing libraries must, in the nature of things, be raised. In an important circular of the 22nd February, 1968 *Bulletin des bibliothèques de France* (April 1968) the director surveyed the whole field of operations and priorities. He pointed out that *communes* of up to 20,000 persons must now be served, the previous limit being 15,000. Efforts should be directed at the growing urban centres, with deposit stations in community centres rather than schools. *Bibliobus* services were a vital factor; the response generated would lead to demands for branch libraries. The grouping of schools would enable larger numbers of children to be reached; special services for such readers would then be developed.

MOBILE LIBRARY OPERATION, URBAN AND RURAL

Many municipalities followed the lead of Grenoble, which put its first urban bibliobus into service in 1956. Often a secondhand vehicle was converted at fairly low cost. Blois, for example, secured a 1951 Chausson bus for F800. Converted, provided with a translucent roof, and shelved at the sides it carried 2,500 books.

Some examples of bibliobus capacity are listed:

Local authority	Vehicle	Books carried
Créteil	Saviem sm 6	2,500
Caen	Citroën long chassis	2,000
Rheims	Saviem	2,300
Ivry-sur-Seine	Berliet Stradair 30	3,500

New vehicles cost between F50,000 and F65,000 and conversion costs have tended to rise rapidly. The costs of a new mobile library for Saint-Etienne were:

vehicle	F62,408
equipment	20,000
initial book stock	40,000
	122,408 (1968 figures)

The stocks carried are roughly one third each of fiction, non-fiction and children's books. Adjustments are made to suit local conditions. Mulhouse carries books in German for German speakers. North African and Polish readers in the Pas-de-Calais are offered books in their own languages.

In Neuilly-sur-Seine the mobile library makes eight halts and has replaced two small branches. Town centres and factory gates are favourite locations.

The attractions of the mobile library service are obvious. They are less expensive than branch libraries and can be put into service much more quickly. Each covers a wider area than the fixed service point. The lower initial cost is of great importance to municipalities which are short of credits. Publicity is another strong attraction, and the town can be seen to be doing something about its library when a large *bibliobus* appears in the streets and visits the local trade fairs.

However, the disadvantages are equally apparent. Choice is limited. The reader cannot indulge in *lecture sur place*. It has been suggested that the rural libraries, having experienced dis-

73

heartening results from deposit stations, are now having too much of a success with the mobile service, in the sense that the very small staff can too easily be overwhelmed by the weight of inescapable routine tasks.

Some feel that the *bibliobus* should be in the nature of a recruiting sergeant to awaken the habit of reading. It should be a first step only, the second being the provision of a fixed branch, sited according to the needs revealed by the mobile service.

Bibliothèques centrales de prêt

Building programme: new headquarters (offices, garages, book stores, etc)

1965	Bas Rhin	1,055 square metres
	Hérault	850
	Loiret	500
	La Réunion	500
	Rhône	1,000
1966	Aveyron	500
	Doubs	500
	Seine-Maritime	500
1967	Dordogne	500
	Ille-et-Vilaine	500
	Ariege	375
1968	Aube	500 To be in service late 1970
	Charente-Maritime	450 „ „ „ 1970
	Marne	900 In service February, 1970

Bibliothèques centrales de prêt

	Local library association established	BCP created
Aisne		1945
Alpes-Maritime	1949	1965
Ariège	1954	1962

	Local library association established	BCP created
Aube	1949	1965
Aveyron		1964
Bouches-du-Rhône		1946
Cantal	1953	1962
Charente	1948	1966
Charente-Maritime	1950	1965
Cher		1964
Corrèze		1967
Corse	1952	1961
Côte-d'Or		1964
Dordogne		1945
Doubs/Territoire de Belfort		1964
Drôme	1948	1965
Eure		1956
Haute-Garonne		1946
Gironde		1946
Hérault		1946
Ille-et-Vilaine		1964
Indre-et-Loire		1946
Isère		1945
Loir-et-Cher		1945
Loire-Atlantique		1968
Loiret	1953	1964
Lot-et-Garonne		1957
Lozère	1953	1965
Manche		1966
Marne		1945
Mayenne		1968
Meurthe-et-Moselle	1948	1968
Meuse	1950	1965
Morbihan		1967
Moselle		1951
Pas-de-Calais	1956	1966
Basses-Pyrénées		1968

	Local library association established	BCP created
Hautes-Pyrénées		1966
Bas-Rhin		1946
Haut-Rhin		1945
Rhône-Ain		1946
Sarthe		1968
Seine-Maritime		1946
Seine-et-Marne	1952	1968
Deux-Sèvres		1945
Somme		1967
Tarn		1945
Seine-et-Oise-Yvelines		1946
Val-d'Oise		1968

FURTHER READING

Descaves, R: ' BCP; quelques nouvelles constructions '. *Bulletin des bibliothèques de France,* July 1969.

'Lecture publique rurale' *in* volume II of the *Cahiers des bibliothèques de France.* Paris, BN, 1956.

' Les bibliothèques centrales de prêt, 1961-66. Analyse comparative des statistiques. *Bulletin des bibliothèques de France,* July 1967.

' Les bibliothèques centrales de prêt : statistiques 1967 et 1968 '. *Bulletin des bibliothèque de France,* January 1970.

Pons, J : ' Les bibliobus urbains en France '. *Bulletin des bibliothèques de France,* February / March 1963.

CHAPTER NINE

University libraries

With the exception of a few institutions of university rank, mainly catholic, higher education in France is entrusted to the state universities.

The country is divided into academic districts, each of which has a university. At the time of writing, however, the number of universities is about to be heavily increased.

The traditional universities were to be found in sixteen academies. These were:

Aix-Marseille founded	1409	
Besançon	1485	
Bordeaux	1441	
Caen	1432	
Clermont-Ferrand	1808	
Dijon	1722	
Grenoble	1339	
Lille	1530:	1888
Lyon	1808	
Montpellier	1289	
Nancy	1572	
Paris	1150	
Poitiers	1431	
Rennes	1735	
Strasbourg	1621	
Toulouse	1230	

More recently the number has risen to twenty two with the addition of Amiens, Limoges, Nice, Orléans, Rheims and Rouen. Some overseas institutions are associated with the French university system.

The teaching faculties are arts (*lettres et sciences humaines*), law and economics, science, medicine and pharmacy.

The universities of France have a long and distinguished history. In the twelfth century Peter Abelard and William of Champeau moved from the precincts of Notre Dame and set up their ' community of masters and scholars ' in the rue St Jacques on the left bank of the Seine. The great religious houses, however, remained vital centres of learning and built up great collections. The Jesuit college of Louis-le-Grand had 50,000 books.

At the time of the revolution the Sorbonne had 28,000 volumes and the university of Douai was equally well endowed. Other university libraries, though, did not profit from the revolutionary confiscations. The contents of the *depôts littéraires* were for the most part already allocated by the time higher education was reorganised in 1808. Only the Sorbonne and the medical faculties of Paris and Montpellier have important stocks of early books. Nor was the build up in modern works too satisfactory. In 1865 there were only 348,782 volumes in French universities at a time when German universities had two million.

Many university buildings were erected in the last quarter of the nineteenth century. The libraries were mostly nonfunctional and incapable of expansion. The 1914-18 war brought destruction and disruption to their services, and between the wars only two universities were able to have new buildings, those of Nancy and Lyon. Most libraries were over-crowded, with books standing two deep and even three deep on the shelves.

In the second world war the university library in Caen was devastated and the national and university library of Strasbourg was partially destroyed. Other great collections were affected, due to serious losses of books and manuscripts. Many were confiscated, others suffered from damp and neglect.

A daunting situation, therefore, faced the newly created *Direction* in 1945. It was required to reconstruct and reequip university libraries at a time of financial difficulty and against the background of a sharp and continuing rise in student numbers. The pressure was inexorable. The following chart shows the climbing attendance figures:

Year	Students
1914	4,200
1939	80,000
1949	116,000
1968	508,119

The university of Paris alone attracted 152,664 students in 1968. The *Direction's* programme aimed to repair war damage and to:

increase book storage areas;

generalise the use of standard adjustable shelves;

increase the number of reading room seats;

provide, where they were lacking, halls with card catalogues and bibliographical aids;

improve the range of periodicals collections;

provide more adequate and better equipped staff working space;

improve lighting, heating and ventilation;

speed up internal communications by means of elevators and book hoists.

University libraries had long been general collections capable of providing books and periodicals for all disciplines. They were, as the French say, ' encyclopedic '. This useful arrangement lasted until a rapidly rising birthrate, and a system which gives all *baccalauréats* an assured place in the university, led to an unbearable congestion in the older university buildings.

By the 1950's the constituent faculties began a process of escaping from antiquated city centre premises to steel, concrete and glass constructions on campus areas beyond the city limits. At the time there was a concentration of interest in science and it was the science faculties which were most active in finding alternative accommodation. Science libraries are very much in the majority when the building programme of the *Direction* is examined. From 1955 to 1967 the comparative figures are:

new science libraries	21
new arts libraries	5
new arts/law libraries	3
new law libraries	4

new medical libraries	5
new *centres hospitalier universitaire*	2
new general libraries	2

The normal pattern follows that to be found in Bordeaux. In 1964 a new science library was built at Talence some way out of the city. It offered 5,170 square metres of library space. In this particular case the separate arts and law faculties were built at Pessac; the two campus areas are cut diagonally by a main road. However this conjunction is not always possible, and there are many cases of faculties being separated by large distances. The new science library at Annapes (1967; 7,920 square metres), near Lille, is a considerable distance away from the city.

Yet another pattern is to be discerned in Aix-Marseille where the law and arts faculties have remained in Aix itself. Sciences have concentrated powerfully in the much larger city of Marseille. The facilities include:

Saint-Charles science library	1958	5,650 square metres
Medical library	1958	2,680
Luminy science library	1967	5,100
St Jérôme science library	1967	4,030
CHU Nord	1969	1,050

The city of Lyon has a large science library in Villeurbanne, away from the crowded commercial area. Inaugurated in 1964, it provided 12,430 square metres.

The science library in Grenoble is some three kilometres from the city. At the time of writing it is the largest science library in France and provides 13,500 square metres of floor space. It is very much a ' *bâtiment de prestige* ', is well planned and was built between 1965 and 1967. There are three student reading rooms with a total of over 1,500 places. Senior students and staff have three more reading rooms with a further five hundred seats.

Near Paris, the science faculty at Orsay was brought into service in 1962 with a library area of 7,920 square metres. A large new extension of 2,000 square metres is about to be added.

The library of the Sorbonne itself has a very large and very rich stock of over $1\frac{1}{2}$ million books in the arts and the sciences.

Its various reading rooms and annexes can accommodate almost a thousand readers. It is, however, primarily a great research library. Undergraduate readers are served by such centres as those of Censier, Nanterre, Dauphine and Vincennes.

The oldest and best known medical library is that of the *Faculté de Médecine* of the University of Paris. Founded in 1733, it originally occupied the sacristy in the chapel of the old medical faculty. It has now become one of the most celebrated of medical collections. In addition to large modern collections in medicine, surgery and biology, it possesses a large number of manuscripts and early treatises. A large new reading room has been added, and good photo-copying facilities are available.

The library of *L'Académie de Médecine* is another vital institution in French medical librarianship. It was founded in 1847. Although reserved for the use of the academy, it is available to approved research workers.

Other useful collections are to be found in INSERN (*Institut National de la Santé et de la Recherche Médicale*), the *Institut Pasteur*, the *Centre Internationale de l'Enfance* and the *Bibliothèque Centrale de l'Internat* of the *Assistance Publique* of Paris.

The medical section of the *Bibliothèque Nationale et Universitaire* at Strasbourg is one of the best of the French medical libraries. Faced with overcrowded reading rooms in the main building, the administrator moved his medical books and periodicals to a new building, in 1965, near the civil hospital in one of Strasbourg's most picturesque areas. The new building offers 1,300 square metres of space and a large stack which will hold 300,000 books. There are 200/250 reading room places. The collection is particularly strong in the history of medicine.

The most pressing problem facing the medical libraries is that of serving the rapidly expanding number of students. The most usual arrangement, that of having the medical/pharmaceutical library in the same building, can be seen in Amiens, Caen, Nantes, Orléans (Tours), Poitiers, Rheims and Rouen. Libraries devoted exclusively to medicine will be found in Bordeaux, Montpellier, Nancy, Rennes, Strasbourg and Toulouse.

In Paris, Lille and Marseille there are examples of the *centre hospitalier et universitaire,* the CHU. These were started in 1958 to coincide with a reformation of medical studies. The intention was to create a closer organisational link between the care of patients, the teaching of medicine and medical research. In Paris the first units were placed near to a group of hospitals. *St-Antoine, la Pitié-Salpêtrière* and *Cochin* are examples. In Grenoble the new medical faculty was built close to a hospital. In *Marseille-Nord* and at *Kremlin-Bicêtre,* in Paris, hospital, teaching and research facilities were organised in the same building. In Lille the principles of the CHU had been anticipated when the *cité hospitalière* had been opened in 1952.

Many of the existing university medical libraries are in cramped, overcrowded quarters awaiting their turn to move to more spacious premises. The new buildings improve teaching conditions and permit better contact between staff and students. Small seminar activities become possible.

The original programme envisaged the creation of twenty two CHU in the provinces. It has recently been decided to organise libraries in no less than ten centres in Paris.

The general administrative offices of a group of university libraries is often located in the humanities or humanities/law libraries. This arrangement will be found in Aix, Amiens, Besançon and elsewhere.

Grenoble provides an example of a large new law and humanities library with a total area of 11,500 square metres. It opened in 1967, building work having begun in 1964. It caters for about 7,000 students from the two faculties and has about 500 reading room seats. The administrative offices are on the first floor and so separate the reading rooms of the younger students from those of senior students and staff.

Another large undertaking in this sector is to be found at Nanterre where there are 20,000 students in the law and arts faculties, and the library here provides 20,300 square metres.

The administrative basis of the university libraries had remained virtually unchanged since the issuing of the *instructions de 1878*. These laid emphasis on conserving the books in a stack where the arrangement was by format and date of accession. Readers had no access to the books which were brought to them by the *gardiens*. The time-honoured rules were, clearly, not designed for the situation of rapid expansion in which the universities found themselves.

The *Direction*, therefore, after full discussions, issued its *instructions* of the 20th June 1962. These moved in the direction of informal open access and laid down standard cataloguing procedures. They decided in favour of the UDC classification for all except medical libraries.

A distinction was drawn between the different needs of junior and senior students, which affected the interior design of libraries built subsequently. The student in his first ' cycle ' and the early part of the second ' cycle ' was chiefly in need of general introductions, course books and non specialised works of reference. These might require to be heavily duplicated. On the other hand the more advanced students, the teaching staff and research workers needed a wider range of more specialised materials.

It was decided that the younger students were to have reading rooms of the traditional type, but these were now to have many open shelves on which both reference and loan copies were to be available without formality. Such rooms were to be, normally, on the ground floor.

On the upper floor or floors the space available was to be divided, informally, into subject areas—*secteurs specialisés*—by means of low bookshelves which were to carry reference books, periodicals and the more recent additions to the bookstock. Items more than two years old and the more specialised books were to be in the stack but available on demand.

The university of Nancy, *section lettres*, which dates from 1964, is a good example of the new approach. There is a basement stack of 940 square metres. On the ground floor the centre of the stack continues to become the backbone of the long rectangular building. Two reading rooms, one on either side of the stack, accommodate 480 readers. The upper floor places 1,230 square metres at the disposal of the advanced users.

What with the normal expansion and the 'reforms of 1962', the building effort has been extremely large and complicated. Since 1955 sixty four new libraries have been provided with a total floor area of 246,000 square metres. Taking into account credits made in 1968 and 1969, there are a further twenty one libraries in the pipeline, with a combined floor area of 93,000 square metres. By the end of 1972, therefore, eighty five new libraries will have been put into service. Most of the projects are for medium sized libraries, but, as we have seen, there are several very large projects in the programme.

Whatever may be the changes of emphasis in the future, the new buildings have an immense advantage over their city centre forerunners. They are all capable of extension when circumstances require. In addition, internal planning takes into account the need for maximum access to the shelves and also for group work and seminar discussions.

In its staffing arrangements the *Direction* has done its best to secure adequate budget allocations for new posts. 1958 university library postings totalled 631. The total for 1969 was 2,422.

University library funds are provided by the *Direction* from the budget of the Ministry of Education. The subvention is for operating costs and bookfunds. Staff members are paid by the state since they form part of the *corps* of librarians. An important secondary source of money is provided by the requirement that each student should pay an annual library fee.

It is not easy to summarise university library arrangements at the present time since large scale alterations in the whole structure of university education are imminent.

The student disorders of 1968 were followed by a new *loi d'orientation*. This seeks to give the staff and students a democratic voice in the affairs of the university. It also aims to break down the very large universities into smaller units in which teaching and research will be integrated. For example, it is currently suggested that the sprawling University of Paris will become a group of thirteen universities. In addition, it has been decided that a university should not be restricted to a single discipline; the concept of *pluridisciplinarité* is strongly urged.

This, of course, means that certain libraries may require to revert to that encyclopedic role which they originally played before the expansion period

In June 1969 discussions on an official level reported in the *Bulletin des bibliothèques de France* suggest that there might be two types of university library:

(i) inter-university libraries; autonomous institutions with large collections capable of serving several universities.

(ii) university libraries of the present type attached to single universities. These might have committees of management which would perhaps represent the interests of teaching staff, library staff, students and might co-opt members from outside the university.

UNIVERSITY LIBRARIES BUILT SINCE 1955

University	Date	Area in square metres
Caen (central)	1955	9,620
Aix-en-Provence (law)	1957	5,560
Marseille (medical)	1958	2,680
Marseille Saint-Charles (science)	1958	5,650
Paris (law)	1958	6,800
Rennes (law) (extension and improvements)	1960	5,500
Sainte-Geneviève, Paris (extension)	1961	4,250
Orsay (science)	1962	7,920
Dijon (central)	1962	5,080
Nice (science)	1964	3,100
Poitiers (science)	1964	4,740
Strasbourg (medical)	1964	3,500
Rouen (law/humanities)	1964	2,140
Lyon (science)	1964	12,430
Bordeaux (science)	1964	5,170
Nancy (humanities)	1965	5,350
Rheims (science)	1965	3,100
Tours (science)	1965	1,200
Le Mans (science)	1965	1,000

	Date	Area in square metres
Paris Censier (humanities)	1965	3,500
Paris CHU St Antoine	1965	800
Toulouse (science)	1965	5,260
Reims (medical)	1966	750
Montpellier (humanities)	1966	5,450
Montpellier (science)	1966	5,240
Paris CHU La Pitié	1966	1,090
Nantes (medical)	1966	2,420
Clermont-Ferrand (law)	1966	1,570
Nantes (science)	1967	4,500
Clermont-Ferrand (humanities)	1967	490
Marseille-Luminy (science)	1967	5,100
Grenoble (law/humanities)	1967	11,500
Besançon (science)	1967	2,810
Aix-en-Provence (humanities)	1967	5,260
Marseille Saint-Jérôme (science)	1967	4,030
Clermont-Ferrand (medical)	1967	2,980
Lille (science)	1967	7,920
Perpignan (science)	1967	900
Orléans (law/humanities)	1967	2,530
Rennes (humanities) (phase I)	1967	5,010
Rennes (science)	1967	5,090
Grenoble (science)	1967	13,500
Pau (science)	1967	2,000
Caen (science)	1968	3,260
Strasbourg (science)	1968	5,480
Tours (medical)	1968	1,100
Nantes (humanities)	1968	3,500
Limoges (science)	1968	1,150
Rennes (medical)	1968	2,100
Bordeaux (law/humanities)	1968	10,000
Rouen (science)	1968	2,700
Grenoble (medical)	1968	1,800
Nice (humanities)	1968	4,500

	Date	Area in square metres
Brest (law/humanities)	1968	3,500
Paris Centre Dauphine	1968	4,600
Paris CHU Cochin	1968	460
Paris Vincennes	1969	2,600
Paris CHU Necker	1969	980
Paris Nanterre (law/humanities) (phase I)	1969	2,200
Toulouse (medical)	1969	4,400
Marseille CHU Nord	1969	1,050
Dijon (medical)	1969	1,500
Saint-Etienne (humanities/science)	1969	2,100
Montpellier (pharmacy)	1969	3,300
Rennes (humanities) (phase II)	1969	5,000
St Maur des Fosses	1969	1,760
Paris St Denis	1969	800
CHU Creteil	1969	1,900
Paris (medical) (extension)	1970	2,400
Paris Nanterre	1970	20,300
Rennes (humanities) (phase II)	1970	5,000
Orsay (science) (extension)	1970	2,000
Clermont-Ferrand (science) (extension)	1970	4,500
Nantes (law)	1970	3,800
Lyon-Bron-Parilly (phase I)	1970	4,000
Lille (pharmacy)	1970	1,500
Rouen (law/humanities) (extension)	1970	2,200
Poitiers (medical)	1970	750
Nice (medical)	1970	850
Brest (medical)	1970	995
Metz	1971	2,000
La Réunion	1971	1,000
Grenoble (medical) (extension)	1971	700
Nancy (science)	1971	5,800
Poitiers (humanities)	1971	10,000
Chambery	1971	900

BUILDING PROGRAMME 1955-1971

Year	Library area added
1955	9,620 square metres
1956	—
1957	5,560
1958	15,130
1959	—
1960	5,500
1961	4,250
1962	13,000
1963	—
1964	31,080
1965	20,210
1966	16,520
1967	73,620
1968	44,150
1969	20,690
1970	50,195
1971	20,400

FURTHER READING

Cahiers des bibliothèques de France. Paris, *Bibliothèque Nationale*. I *Bibliothèques universitaires*, 1954. II *Les bibliothèques et l'université*, 1957.

Poindron, P: 'French university libraries'. *Library Trends*, XII (4) 1964.

Bulletin des bibliothèques de France:
' University library statistics 1954/5 ' October 1956;
' University library statistics 1955/6-1959-60, December 1961;
' Science libraries—reorganisation ', May 1961;
' Conference on university libraries, 1961 ', February 1962;
' Libraries in *centres hospitaliers et universitaires*', February 1968;
' Clermont-Ferrand, new library ', May 1967;
' Clermont-Ferrand, new medical library ', December 1968;
' Dijon, new university library ', July 1963;
' Grenoble, new buildings ', April 1969;

' Nancy, new *section lettres* library ', April 1968;
' Orsay, new science library ', December 1962;
' Poitiers, new science library ', September/October 1964;
' Rennes, new university library ', December 1960;
' Rheims, new science library ', April 1967.

CHAPTER TEN

Library methods

The interior planning of large numbers of French library buildings is such that they cannot easily be adjusted to accommodate
new methods. Even the university library policy set out in the
circular of June 1962 has not been carried out completely, it
would appear. This emerged from the May 1968 conference of
the French library association at Clermont-Ferrand. The inhibit-
ing factors had been the continuing shortages of staff, space and
money. However, since more new buildings were coming into use,
a comparison of methods was possible. Information from 132
libraries of all types was pooled, and conclusions on the following
subjects were reached.

Open access to stack areas

In university libraries teaching staff have free access. This is,
however, not the case in the municipal libraries where such
access is exceptional. Many libraries reported abuses of such
privileged treatment.

Students have no such rights. In some libraries, however, part
of the stack has been thrown open to permit access to course
textbooks for first and second year students.

Stock losses

Though there are libraries which have no problem, others are
worried. The question of whether or not to control briefcases is
a controversial issue.

Advice to readers

This is generally possible at all times in the *bibliothèques
universitaires*. In the more recent buildings a librarian or sub-
librarian is at work behind a plate glass screen in a small office
on the reading room floor but available for consultation. In the
library of the pharmacy faculty, in Paris, such advice is available
from a *conservateur*.

In smaller libraries, however, such help might come from the head of the service staff or, perhaps, the assistant who looks after inter-library loans. Many municipal libraries, however, have no member of staff free to explain the use of the library or to offer help in the selection of books.

Law faculties are favoured in that practical work figures in the timetable. This enables some law libraries to brief readers on the library service and to introduce the main bibliographical aids. In the libraries of the humanities, however, there is no obligation to attend such sessions.

Generally speaking, comparatively few libraries provide written guides to the collections. A recent survey (1969) indicated that twenty out of a total of fifty four university or learned libraries circulated one. In the public library group thirty three libraries out of ninety six had one. On the other hand most libraries are in favour of making this provision.

The duration of home loans
The average duration of loans is:
Municipal libraries
    Home lending sections 2 to 3 weeks
    Study library sections   4 weeks
University libraries
    Reference books   week-end issues
    Periodicals   8 days
    Books; for students   2 weeks
    Books; for staff   4 weeks

Fines for late returns
Municipal libraries have the law behind them. They may charge fines and may send municipal officials out in search of missing books. University libraries, on the other hand, may not legally charge fines. The rates in the municipalities vary from Fo.01 per day to F1 per week. The university librarians threaten to report offenders or suspend them. In some cases the reminders go out from the office of the head of the department. Some extreme action is possible; a student's file could be held up and this would preclude him sitting an examination.

Photocopying

Apparatus is now common in the university libraries but there are many municipal libraries which are not equipped. They use commercial services or the town hall machine. Charges to users vary from Fo.30 to F1 per frame. The average is Fo.50 in universities and F1 in municipal libraries. A few libraries offer a free service if only a few pages require to be copied.

Postal borrowing

Postal loans to readers who cannot visit the library are rare in France. They occur from time to time where a student falls sick or is otherwise handicapped. One university library contrives to serve distant teachers by lending to the nearby CRDP unit. Since this has a free postal service it obligingly acts as post office.

Reference book loans

Most municipal libraries and older university libraries lend reference books at week-ends, although only exceptionally and to known readers. The consent of the chief librarian is often necessary. In the newer university libraries there is, it seems, more flexibility. Of the sample:

5 libraries did not lend

25 libraries lent habitually

8 libraries lent exceptionally.

Control of book loans

Most municipal libraries used the Newark or the Browne book charging methods and photocharging is apparently not used at all. A few libraries use taperecorders. University libraries tend to use systems involving signed slips.

Classification systems

Nearly all municipal libraries use the Dewey decimal scheme and it is recommended by many of the cultural organisations concerned with private libraries in community centres and youth clubs. Work is currently in progress on an adaptation of the Dewey system for France. This is a collaboration between a group of librarians in Lyon and Canadian librarians.

The UDC scheme is adopted in most new university libraries and some old ones. It is also employed in a handful of municipal libraries.

Medical sections of university libraries and the medical school libraries, the CHU, use either the classification of the National Library of Medicine or the Cunningham scheme.

The Library of Congress scheme is used in the library of the *Musée de l'Homme*.

Some additional points not covered by the proceedings of the Clermont-Ferrand conference are added.

Binding problems

Most French books are bound in paper wrappers. Limited books funds are further reduced by the need to provide hard covers which are costly. However, useful slip cases made from transparent plastic are now on the market. Popular libraries are under some compunction to duplicate prize winning novels and non-fiction books. During the period of their popularity they are circulated in the slip cases. For permanent retention only one or two copies are selected for rebinding. There are many libraries with their own small binderies.

Accession registers

These are generally maintained and are recommended in the various manuals for privately organised libraries. There is a standardised ruling for the accession register, *Norme française* 2/4500/1.

Library membership

Some comment may be made on the recent changes in the composition of the readership in municipal libraries. In the past the main users were the older readers and retired people. Reference libraries were the preserve of elderly research workers.

The city of Paris and other systems now report that the balance is altering. Young people aged betwen sixteen and thirty make up fifty percent of the membership. Middle class readers are much in evidence—a significant change in attitude, though children's libraries reach readers with widely differing social backgrounds.

One of the most radical changes, however, has been the invasion of the reading rooms and the reference libraries by many thousands of university students and, indeed, members of the teaching staffs. This situation seems to arise from the fact that many university libraries are short of reading room places. One seat for each ten students has been suggested as the norm, but this is not always achieved. In addition, the university is often unable to meet the book demands of the users. There are doubtless occasions, too, when the campus is at a distance from the city centre, and this may discourage some university readers from making unnecessary journeys.

Computers and data processing

By 1968 twenty three major documentation centres were using computers and the *Centre National de la Recherche Scientifique* controls its periodicals acquisitions in this way. The proposed *annexe* of the BN at Les Halles and the very large new city library at Lyon will use data processing methods; these have already been applied to the task of producing a catalogue of the early printed and rare books in French municipal libraries.

LIBRARY TECHNICAL JOURNALS AND VOCABULARY

It is not too difficult to follow the argument in French library journals. For difficult technical terms use: *Vocabularium bibliothecarii,* Unesco, 1962.

The main sources are:

Association des Bibliothécaires Français: Bulletin d'informations.

Bibliographie de la France (2nd section, Chronique).

Bulletin des bibliothèques de France.

Documentaliste.

Lecture et bibliothèques.

CHAPTER ELEVEN

Interlibrary cooperation

There are many cases of cooperation, voluntary or otherwise, in French library history. The city library at Lille was given a home in the university library when the municipal library was destroyed. In Lyon the municipal library sheltered the *bibliothèque centrale de prêt* for the region until new premises were provided. The city centre premises of the university of Grenoble were handed over for municipal use. One reads of museum premises being made available for a municipal library book week. Such flexibility is praiseworthy, although the situation is often the result of an insufficient number of the right kind of buildings for the purpose in mind.

Cooperation with other organisations is an important part of the new approach to public library work recommended in the 1968 report. An example of this spirit at work is to be found in the activities of the *Office Socio-Culturel* established in Pau. This city, with 61,468 inhabitants, is growing rapidly; half of the area is given over to new housing developments. From the start of the work of the new organisation the chief librarian was associated fully; this has resulted in close contact with the library, and demands for a mobile library service on the part of nearby communities.

Some cooperative ventures are of long standing, one example being the *Service des Echanges Universitaires*. This useful bureau was organised in the Sorbonne library. It collects theses from all French universities and exchanges them for the publications of foreign institutions which are, in turn, distributed.

University library cooperation is often concerned with union catalogues. In 1918 the University of Montpellier made an alphabetical list of periodicals in the possession of university libraries in France, with the exception of Lille and Paris. Work in this field continues in the *Catalogue collectif des périodiques du début du XVIIe siècle à 1939 conservés dans les bibliothèques de Paris et dans les bibliothèques universitaires des départements* (+ supplements). This publication includes entries from about seventy five libraries and has entries for about 75,000 French and foreign periodicals.

A similar publication which relies on the help of very many library staffs is the publication known as ' IPPEC '. This is the *Inventaire permanent des périodiques étrangers en cours*. The *Direction* decided in 1952 to have a union catalogue of foreign current periodicals in libraries and documentation centres. The number of entries has grown rapidly since the first edition was published in 1957. The fourth edition has been produced by computer.

In order to build up the *Catalogue collectif des ouvrages étrangers*, the university libraries send slips to Paris representing their non French books. The CCOE catalogue is kept in the national library and is the main source for information on books from about 1950 onwards.

There are some examples of stocks of books held in common. The faculty of medicine in Paris has loan stocks for the use of other schools of medicine. At Orsay, a stock of recent science books has been built up and is available on loan as a result of the work of the *Service d'Information Bibliographique*. This latter institution was organised to assist university librarians to select acquisitions. It was of special value at a time when many university colleges of science were being established. However, these reservoir stocks do not provide a sufficiently large reserve for the inter-lending services.

Inter-loans in the university library sector date from 1886. Free postal facilities were granted in 1887, and as a result of various subsequent regulations inter-lending was extended to the other libraries and, indeed, the university libraries are able to take part in the general service.

In addition to the lack of a centralised stock of books available for loan mentioned above, one must add the fact that there is no large national or regional catalogue. The loan service, therefore, tends to be a slow process.

The *Service Central des Prêts* of the national library is in charge of inter-loan work. It was originally intended to deal with the lending of manuscripts and rare works. With a small staff, it must now contend with a rising number of enquiries for recent or fairly recent works. Non French books can be checked in the *Catalogue collectif des ouvrages étrangers*.

For other requests the *Service Central* has access to duplicates in the stock of the *Bibliothèque National*. In addition, there is a partial catalogue of annual additions to the collections in university libraries reinforced by cards from other collections. If no entry can be found the request may be referred to an appropriate special library. Alternatively it may be included in a ' wants ' list sent out regularly to about 120 libraries.

FURTHER READING

Congrès ABF (Dijon): ' Le prêt interbibliothèque ' ABF *Bulletin d' informations* 56 (3) 1967.

Nortier, M: ' Le prêt entre bibliothèques en France '. *Bulletin des bibliothèques de France*, April/May 1965.

CHAPTER TWELVE

Library profession

STRUCTURE: The state organisation of library posts is so arranged that clear distinctions are drawn between professional, technical and service duties. There are four main divisions of staff. They are:

Category A: The *corps scientifique* responsible for management and administration.
The posts are graded:
conservateur-en-chef de classe exceptionelle
conservateur-en-chef
conservateur—1st class
conservateur—2nd class

Category B: The *corps technique* responsible for all technical processes. Posts are graded:
sous-bibliothécaire, chef de section
sous-bibliothécaire de classe exceptionelle
sous-bibliothécaire

Category C: The *corps des magasiniers* who are concerned with control and management of the books and materials. Posts are graded:
chef magasinier principal
chef magasinier
magasinier

Category D: The *corps des gardiens* who are concerned with shelf order, the finding of books for readers and the supervision of public rooms. There is one grade only.

The staffing situation in the municipal libraries is more complex. Librarians and certain senior staff members in ' classified ' public libraries are members of the state library staff.

In the unclassified libraries the grades are:
bibliothécaire;
sous-bibliothécaire;
employé de bibliothèque;
surveillant de bibliothèque/garçon de bibliothèque.

There are two grades of unclassified library. Candidates for posts as librarians in group one would either be holders of the diploma for *archivistes-paléographes* or graduate holders of the state higher diploma in librarianship. Librarians in group two libraries would either be graduates with the *certificat d'aptitude aux fonctions de bibliothèque* or nongraduate holders of the CAFB who had had experience in librarianship. Municipal *sous-bibliothécaires* normally hold the *baccalauréat* or *brevet supérieur*.

Larger library staffs include such specialists as binders, restorers and a growing body of drivers for the mobile libraries.

EDUCATION
In the latter part of the nineteenth century moves were made to ensure that librarians should possess a professional qualification. In 1880 practical training in librarianship was made available in the *Bibliothèque Sainte-Geneviève*.

In 1882 it was laid down that university librarians should be certificated. In 1893 a *Certificat d'aptitude aux fonctions de bibliothécaire universitaire* was instituted. This was followed by the *Certificat d'aptitude aux fonctions de bibliothécaire dans une bibliothèque municipale classée*.

There were no formal courses which were readily available, although the *École des Chartes* had, in 1869, added regular courses in bibliography and classification.

The *École des Chartes* was founded in 1821, reorganised in 1847 and moved into the Sorbonne in 1879. Its aim was to produce scholars able to work intelligently with source materials on the history of France. Its own library is particularly rich in early materials. Selected students are admitted; a maximum of twenty seven being taken each year. A three year course leads to the *diplôme d'archiviste-paléographe*. The training given, while of the greatest importance to historical research, is not related to the needs of librarians in community libraries. Nevertheless a ministerial decision of 1897 required mayors to select chartists when filling vacancies for municipal chief librarians. In fairness to the chartists, many of them took up the cause of public libraries with great enthusiasm. One could quote the case of Henri Vendel, the celebrated pioneer of the library movement.

The situation, however, was not acceptable to the *Association des Bibliothécaires Français*, which strongly advocated a more practical training. A series of lectures was, therefore, arranged in the *École des Hautes Etudes Sociales* in the period 1911-1914.

Systematic training linked to practical needs came in 1923 and was an American initiative. The schemes for public and rural libraries launched after the 1914-1918 war called for adequately prepared local staff. A six week summer course was arranged by the American Library Association and proved to be so successful that a full time establishment was proposed.

The American Library School in Paris prepared over two hundred librarians between 1923 and 1929, the year in which it closed.

An attempt was made to keep the school alive under the auspices of the city of Paris, but unfortunately the city council found itself unable to raise adequate money to meet the teaching expenses.

The *École de Bibliothécaires* at the *Institut Catholique de Paris* was founded in 1935 by M Gabriel Henriot, a former chief inspector of libraries in the city. This takes a limited number of students, with a maximum of thirty, and provides a two year course leading to a diploma. There is a general cultural background course. The technical aspects of librarianship and documentation are covered, in addition to which groups of students are attached to Paris libraries for practical work. In the second year much attention is given to documentary techniques and to visits to modern documentation centres. An evening course is arranged for working librarians, and the younger students may take a year's preparatory training. The name of the school has recently been altered to *École de Bibliothécaires-Documentalistes.* Even before this initiative, moves were being made to establish a framework of state training. In 1932 the *diplôme technique de bibliothécaire* was instituted to test such library skills as cataloguing, classification, bibliography and administration. This was followed, in 1950, by the *diplôme supérieur de bibliothécaire,* which required a course of more advanced study and was designed to prepare holders for the more senior posts. A third qualification, the *certificat d'aptitude aux fonctions de bibliothécaire* (CAFB), was instituted in 1951 and reformed in 1960. The intention here was to provide a qualification for those responsible for the operations of the smaller libraries.

In addition to a general background course, the candidate may choose an option most appropriate to his career. The present selection is :

institute and laboratory libraries;

school and children's libraries;

municipal libraries;

lecture publique libraries, that is to say, lending sections in municipal libraries, works libraries and rural or BCP libraries.

From 1954 onwards the *Direction* organised short three week courses for the CAFB and the instruction was given in part in the *Bibliothèque Nationale.* Duplicated course notes were provided.

It was not until 1964, however, that the long hoped for library school was established by the state. This is the *École Nationale Supérieure de Bibliothécaires.* It has temporary premises opposite the *Bibliothèque Nationale* in rue de Louvois. Its director is *Mlle* Paule Salvan. In addition to the provision of a course leading to the *diplôme supérieur de bibliothécaire,* it also provides instruction leading to the *diplôme technique* and the CAFB.

During 1968-69 the various courses were provided as follows:

Subject	Instruction (*hours*)	Practical work (*hours*)	Visits (*hours*)
History of the book and printing	33	24	5
Bibliography	28	12	
History of libraries	6		
Library administration	9	4	
Library economy	27	16	
National libraries	4	8	
University libraries	20	2	5
Public libraries	24	4	5
Documentation	29	4	8
Cataloguing	9	63	
Options:			
Historical bibliography	2	9	
Abstracts		6	
Lecture publique		15	

Candidates for the higher diploma must be graduates and under thirty years of age. They sit a competitive entrance examination. A second entrance examination is open to those who, aged between twenty five and thirty five have had five years' service in the rank of sub-librarian. Successful candidates become *élèves bibliothécaires* and receive a grant of just over F1,000 a month; F1,238 with various state and family additions. Some additional places are available for those who do not hold French qualifications. The ' associated students ' receive no grant and pay class fees.

Successful candidates receive the *diplôme supérieur* and have two months' attachment to one or other of the large specialist libraries. Thereafter they are posted to one of the establishments under the care of the *Direction*. This posting takes account of the candidate's interests and his placing in the examination lists. After a year on probation the holder of the higher diploma may expect to be placed on the first *échelon* of the scale relating to *conservateurs.* Students, other than associated students, engage to serve in the libraries of the *Direction* for ten years.

Holders of arts degrees are most heavily represented among the intake. Though science librarians are much in demand, comparatively few science graduates have, so far, joined the courses. Admissions for 1969 were:

Diplomas possessed	Men	Women
Maitrise	4	2
Diplôme d'études supérieurs	3	2
License—lettres	15	46
Licence—sciences	–	4
Licence—droit	3	1
Five years' service	1	7
	26	62

A six month course is organised in connection with the competitive examinations which lead to an appointment as *sous-bibliothécaire*. Courses are also provided at certain provincial centres if sufficient candidates come forward. There are written and oral examinations, and those declared successful have to complete a further year's practical work in one of the libraries in the care of the *Direction*.

A third course of training is provided for those librarians in Paris who are preparing themselves for the *certificat d'aptitude aux fonctions de bibliothécaire*. The general and specialised training is completed by a working attachment to a library of eighty hours. Provincial candidates are required to work full time for six weeks in an approved municipal library, though a part time attachment for three months is a possible alternative.

As noted elsewhere, when describing municipal library initiatives, it was observed that the ENSB had instituted a public library in Massy. This is used to provide good practical training for library students.

LIBRARY ASSOCIATIONS

Since its foundation in 1906, the *Association des Bibliothécaires Français* has served the cause of libraries in all fields—municipal, national, university and special. Its aims are to bring together all who work in libraries, to study all aspects of librarianship, to promote the development of libraries and to represent the country in the international library organisations.

To this end it arranges meetings, conferences, study tours, courses in library education and other activities. It also publishes the results of enquiries into library operations.

There are several types of membership; in addition to professional full members, those interested in librarianship may become *adhérants*. Institutional membership is encouraged.

There are various regional groups which arrange programmes of meetings and visits. Some of these are: Lorraine, Aquitaine, Bourgogne-Franche-Comté, Ile-de-France and so on.

The specialised needs of members are met by the relevant sections, which include public libraries, special libraries (which has various sub-sections—administrative libraires, art, economics, exact sciences and geology), libraries of biology and medicine, etc.

The association's annual conference allows for the discussion of current problems. It provides training for nonqualified staff in small libraries and has been most active in the struggle to establish a structure of library qualifications.

On the basis of the last published *Annuaire des membres*, the association has about 1,700 members on its lists, of which about twenty seven to thirty percent are male. These are drawn from a wide range of institutions from the national and learned libraries to the popular libraries.

Its *Bulletin d'Informations* is published quarterly, and the public libraries section, which is very active, produces *Lecture et bibliothèques*; a journal which reports progress in this field.

A new organisation, the *Association Nationale des Bibliothécaires Municipaux* made its appearance in 1970 to cater for the special interests of this branch of library service.

There is an organisation to look after the interests of those working in specialised libraries and centres of documentation. It is the *Association des Documentalistes et des Bibliothécaires Spécialisés*.

The *Association de l'École Nationale Supérieure de Bibliothécaires* was founded in 1967 in succession to the *Association des*

Titulaires des Diplômes Supérieurs de Bibliothécaire which dated from 1960. The previous association had taken an active part in the reform of education for librarianship and in the moves to set up a full time school.

The AENSB unites holders of the higher and the technical diplomas and has amongst its aims the encouragement of research into all library problems.

FURTHER READING
Annuaire de l'Association de l'École Nationale Supérieure de Bibliothécaires. ENSB 2 rue de Louvois, Paris 2.

Annuaire 1967 des membres de l' Association des Bibliothécaires Français. ABF, 4 rue de Louvois, Paris 2.

Ministère de l'Education Nationale: *Bureau universitaire de statistique et de documentation scolaires et professionnelles. École Nationale Supérieure de Bibliothécaires. (Doc scolaire notice* 148) December 1969, This is the official handbook to the state library school.

Salvan, P: ' Réforme de la formation professionnelle '. *Bulletin des Bibliothèques de France,* June 1963.

Salvan, P: ' The national school of librarianship in Paris '. *Unesco bulletin for libraries,* XIX (4) 1965.

CHAPTER THIRTEEN

Archives and documentation

The *Archives de France* constitute a magnificent collection which traces the history of the country from Mérovingien times to the present day. A law of 1790 set up the national archives. The present headquarters of the *Direction des Archives de France* are in the famous Hôtels de Soubise and de Rohan in Paris. The directorate is part of the Ministry of Cultural Affairs.

A law of 1796 established departmental archives in the various provincial capitals. The collections were originally placed in the offices of the *préfectures*. As they grew, however, they were for the most part stored and organised in adjacent buildings. Some of the locations were not completely satisfactory. However, a new building programme has provided many modern buildings in the provincial cities.

The educational value of the archives has been recognised and exploited. The museum in the *Hôtel de Soubise* is extremely well organised, and like its counterparts in the regional offices, it attracts many visitors and organised groups from schools.

DOCUMENTATION

In December 1968, the French government set up the *Comité Nationale de la Documentation Scientifique et Technique* to encourage development in this field. The new body must keep in touch with various centres, must coordinate their activities and facilitate exchanges of information. It is intended to encourage new activities including linguistic usage and the standardisation of methods. The *comité* is interested in international cooperation, and has a permanent secretariat at the documentation centre of the CNRS in Paris. The nine permanent members include the director of libraries and the director of the CNRS documentation centre.

The initials CNRS are well known in the scientific world. They stand for the *Centre National de la Recherche Scientifique* which has a large number of specialised scientific centres throughout France. Its documentation centre was established in 1940 to provide scientists, technicians and research workers with whatever scientific papers they might require. It has a very large library of over 13,000 sets of periodicals. Some 7,000 of these together with conference reports and university theses are searched by specialists and the articles analysed and classified. Information is carried to research workers by means of the *Bulletin signalétic*.

The photocopying facilities are extremely well organised and the unit can produce between 1,500 and 3,000 documents daily. Microfilms and other methods of copying are available.

Translations into French are handled by a team of several hundred translators. To prevent duplication the translations are registered daily.

The periodicals in the collection are not lent. Readers may work in the reading room or obtain photocopies. Up to seventy readers can be accommodated in the library.

Some delays are encountered in the production of the *Bulletin signalétique*. To reduce these to a minimum, studies are being made which may permit the use of computer methods. In the same way, efforts are being made to control the receipt of periodicals by mechanical methods. The documentation centre also provides in-service training to documentalists from other countries.

The *Association Nationale de la Recherche Technique* (ANRT) has over 400 institutional or individual members representing some 53,000 research workers and technicians. It meets annually and the work of its ' commissions ' is continuous. The association publishes an information bulletin called *Recherche technique,* and has an active working party on information and documentation. It has produced a *Répertoire des revues techniques pour l'industrie* in association with the *Direction des Bibliothèques* and cooperates with CNRS in the publication of the periodical *Information et documentation*. Good relations have been established with FID and with organisations concerned with documentation in other countries.

In the field of reprography the coordinating body is the *Comité Français de la Reprographie*. Until 1964 there was no national body concerned with this subject. The *comité* brings together the principal interested bodies and acts as correspondent to the various related organisations elsewhere.

At least twenty three of the major documentation centres in France use computer techniques. They include CEA (*Commissariat a l'Energie Atomique*), SNPA (*Société Nationale des Pétroles d'Aquitaine*), and the *Compagnie de Saint-Gobain*. For a full discussion of methods and equipment see the *Liste de quelques services documentaires mécanisés* (*Bulletin des bibliothèques de France*, November 1968).

For full details of documentation centres generally see the *Répertoire des bibliothèques de France*, vol 3 *Centres et services de documentation*, Paris, *Bibliothèque Nationale*, 1951.

The Documentation Centre for Education in Europe has its headquarters in the *Maison de l'Europe* at Strasbourg since it is part of the Directorate of Cultural and Scientific Affairs of the Council of Europe. It has an interest not only in French educational documentation but also in that of the other member countries—Austria, Belgium, Cyprus, Denmark, Federal Germany, Iceland, Ireland, Italy, Netherlands, Norway, Spain, Sweden, Switzerland, Turkey and the United Kingdom. French educational abstracts and other documents are issued by the *Institut Pédagogique National* of Paris.

The development of documentation in France owes a great deal to the pioneering work of the *Union Française des Organismes de Documentation* (UFOD), of Paris. It was founded in 1932 and aimed to bring together those interested in the development of documentation, to determine programmes, to coordinate the various efforts and to concern itself with the training and recruitment of documentalists. It organised courses from 1945 onwards. In 1950 the technical training was transferred to the *Institut National des Techniques de la Documentation*.

This latter institution is one of the institutes of the *Conservatoire National des Arts et Métiers*. A two year course for graduates is provided.

A more recent course is provided in certain university institutes of technology. One of the options in the *Carrières de l'information* is designed to produce documentalists.

FURTHER READING

Ministère de l'Education Nationale: Bureau universitaire de statistique et de documentation scolaires et professionnelles. Institut National des Techniques de la Documentation.

Poindron, P: 'La formation des documentalistes en France'. *Bulletin des Bibliothèques de France,* August 1963.

Répertoire des bibliothèques de France. Centres et services de documentation. Paris, Unesco/Direction des Bibliothèques 1951. This is a very useful systematic list of centres with details of their special features, publications and administrative control. Some 309 institutions are included, of which 248 are in Paris.

CHAPTER FOURTEEN

The present state of
La Lecture Publique

La lecture publique en France is the title of a report by a working
party to an interministerial committee which set about a study
of the means of developing public library work. It was published
in February 1968, by *La Documentation française (Notes et études
documentaires* no 3459) and reprinted in the *Bulletin des bibliothèques de France* in March 1968. It is undoubtedly the most
important document on the subject currently available.

The committee was assembled on the instructions of *M* Georges
Pompidou, who presided over it. Its working group met under
the chairmanship of the Director of Libraries, the municipal
librarian of Tours being a permanent member.

The report began by suggesting that the very expression
'*lecture publique*' was not widely understood. It described the
administrative framework which had been provided—700 municipal libraries, state aid, the legal right to create rural central
libraries and departmental 'associations'. Analysing the extent
to which these met the needs of the day, it found many weaknesses
in comparison with results in other countries.

Less than half the *départements* had been provided with a
service:

	Metropolitan departments	*Communities with less than 15,000 inhabitants*	*Population*
Total to be served	95	37,582	27,762,000
Actually served (1966)	39	16,435	13,681,762

110

Of the 13·6 millions served, 9½ million were in areas served by *bibliobus*. The lack of interest displayed by some unpaid village librarians further reduced the effectiveness of the scheme. Statistics were, naturally, incomplete but it appeared that two to four percent of the adult population and fifty to seventy five percent of the school population used the rural services where these existed.

As far as the larger municipal libraries were concerned, their central libraries, branches and mobile libraries met part only of the needs. In the smaller communities the collections and the buildings were, generally, in poor shape and lacked an adequate number of staff. Of a total population of 15·4 million only 524,000 were registered readers. This provides a figure of about three percent. If account is taken of Paris, the most optimistic figure is 4·6 percent of the total population—a low one when compared with those ranging between twenty and forty percent returned by various other countries. Other disquieting figures related to total book circulation and to overall expenditure:

	France	Canada	USSR	UK	USA	Denmark
Books borrowed per head per annum	·74	5·8	4·5	9·4	5·4	7
Expenditure per head per annum	Fo·65	F6·36	—	F10·5	F12·6	F17·5

Before suggesting remedies the report tried to analyse the reasons for the lack of progress. France had failed to respond sufficiently to the public library movement. Book collections had been enriched at the cost of service in the reading rooms. In the same way, book funds had been spent on conservation and re-binding at the expense of new acquisitions. Librarians had not been trained to attract general readers. Even compulsory education had unhelpful effects in that its development had not been linked to a network of public libraries. To many people books were associated with school work in unattractive surroundings and their eventual rejection became a sign of maturity. Private enterprise libraries had tried to compensate for the partial failure of the official system. Nevertheless the state should retain the honour of providing an example to other agencies.

Where librarians and administrators carried out imaginative programmes the results were immediate and satisfying, as, for example, in Bordeaux, Tours, Yerres (Esonne) and Sarcelles. The report went on to propose measures which if put into action would give that impulse to the library movement which was lacking. To the traditional functions of the *conservateurs* new duties must be added. Readers must be welcomed. Trained librarians should be available as readers' advisers. Programmes of extension activities should be undertaken. Librarians should play an active part in local cultural activities.

A new corps of *bibliothécaires de lecture publique* should be created and special training provided for them in the university institutes of technology.

The requirements for large public libraries were detailed. The traditional arrangement of a very large stack and a very small reading room should be reversed. Special branches for children should be provided. The complex problems of new development areas deserved special study. Opening hours should permit the widest possible access to libraries.

The question of a membership charge was left open though some mayors felt that a small charge was desirable.

In small towns the library had a valuable role. Equipped with a gramophone record library and a hall, it could become a cultural centre. However, many small towns and most villages were unable to start their own library and would require the services of a completed network of BCP rural libraries. Block loans would permit the rejuvenation of existing small municipal libraries. A better service to the fixed points and an improved service of direct issues from the mobile libraries would require a very large fleet; though large costs were involved such a programme was deemed indispensable.

Children's libraries were important since the acquisition of a taste for reading was vital. The ideal solution was a children's library, either independent or linked with the municipal library, but good results could be obtained if the bookmobiles called at schools.

The special problems of housing areas were summarised. To encourage the establishment of libraries the regulations relating to them would be changed to enable municipalities to acquire sites. In new development projects a library should be included for each 5,000 dwellings.

Administrative changes would encourage local authorities in their efforts. It was considered that the time was not ripe for a law which would make it imperative for each municipality to provide a service. They were, however, to be encouraged to create new libraries or to renovate old ones by means of more liberal state aid. New constructions were to attract fifty percent state assistance in place of the previous thirty five percent. Additions would be made to the municipal budget on the following scale:

Municipal expenditure per head	*State subvention*		
F2 to F4	5 percent of local budget		
F4 to F6	10	,,	,,	,,
Upwards of F6	15	,,	,,	,,

New libraries would receive an initial stock. The state ' classification ' would be extended over the next ten years to include other systems, thus giving them the right to state personnel, additional books and the possibility of a mobile library.

Good coordination was imperative because of the number of different government ministries involved (education, youth and sports, cultural affairs, information, interior and defence). Good relations were equally necessary in the regional capitals.

The *Direction* was to be reinforced and more attention was to be given to research and development. Much emphasis was given to the need for publicity for library development.

The special features and problems of the Paris area were analysed with the finding that the city libraries should have a closer link with the national library service.

In conclusion it was admitted that the lost ground was considerable and that it could not be recovered at short notice. Only a long term plan could reach the objectives defined by the working party. A ten year plan, with an indication of financial requirements, had been worked out.

Press reactions to the document were mixed. Some newspapers welcomed an admirably objective and critical appreciation of the current situation but others suggested that the measures advocated were too limited. *La voix de l'édition* (no 82 April 1969 and subsequent numbers) felt that undue reliance had been placed on state encouragement on the one hand and on mobile library services on the other. While welcoming the increased grant towards new buildings it pointed out that many communities would be unable to raise the initial sum needed to attract the state matching grant. Nor could mobile libraries provide that range of services offered by the static library. To leave development in the hands of the municipalities would be dangerous, and it was felt that the provision of a library service should be made obligatory. State aid should be increased and should meet, in some cases, the whole cost of the new structure.

The disorders of May 1968 led to meetings of students, academics and professional people of all types. In the ' spirit of May ' it was fashionable to criticise authority and all administrative structures. Even the readers at the *Bibiolthèque Nationale* formed an association to promote their interests.

In July about 300 librarians met in Paris (*Les assises nationales des bibliothèques*) in order to discuss progress. Though reported in the *Bulletin d'informations* no 61, 1968, of the *Association des Bibliothécaires Français* the conference was in the nature of a spontaneous, but unofficial, professional gathering. It was divided into various commissions which considered difficulties in various spheres of activity. It was proposed that there should be a detailed library development plan and a national lending library. There should be inspectors of libraries in each of the twenty or so economic regions, and a national library council, fully representative of all types of library, should decide on policy.

The university library commission pointed out that university courses less dominated by the ' set piece ' lecture would rely more on the personal work, with library materials, of the individual.

Libraries would have to be strengthened to meet the situation. Seminar rooms were needed in addition to better research facilities. The university library should be autonomous; attached to the *Direction* but with its own committee.

The research librarians referred to recruiting difficulties. With ENSB students going directly into the state libraries they found it difficult to obtain trained staff. They recommended that training facilities should be improved, and urged the retraining of serving librarians, especially in modern documentation and administrative techniques.

It is interesting that the *Commission des Bibliothèques Publiques* was so named. The term '*bibliothèque publique*' is coming into wide use to denote a library in which the emphasis is on service to all. Among other suggestions it adopted the principle of the 'sector library' which would serve a population group of 100,000. There would be a fully equipped *bibliothèque publique centrale* with branches in urban areas. Communities of 3,000 would rate one. Two or more mobile libraries would serve the villages in a radius of forty to fifty kilometres from the central library.

A *bibliothèque régionale de prêt* network could reinforce the municipal and BCP services. It would concern itself with regional cooperation, interlending, library education, the proper organisation of the documents of the region, and would have a specialised service for the rare books of the area.

Better children's libraries were essential and these were not to be isolated from those of adults. Library skills should be taught at all academic levels. All educational establishments should have libraries, these being in the care of trained teacher-librarians. The majority of hospital libraries should be branches of municipal libraries.

Summing up, it called for a law which would define the various duties of the local and national authorities on the one hand and would assure, on the other, the right of all citizens to a library service.

Since the events of 1968 much quietly effective work has been done to put the additional credits, which followed in the wake of the working party report, to good use.

There has been a considerable increase in the size of the municipal library building programme. As has been indicated elsewhere, the new city library in Lyon will be the largest yet erected by the *Direction*. Those new libraries to be put into service in Caen, Tarbes, Bron, Creil, and elsewhere are also reasonably large undertakings.

The rural library programme is, similarly, beginning to move at a more rapid pace. It is interesting to compare 1967 and 1968 levels in the *bibliothèque centrale de prêt* facilities to urban and rural districts.

	1967	*1968*
New BCP libraries created	Corrèze	Mayenne
	Morbihan	Meurthe-et-Moselle
	Somme	Basses-Pyrénées
		Sarthe
		Seine-et-Marne
		Val-d'Oise
		Loire Atlantique
Total book stocks:	2,675,043	3,264,701
Bibliobus vehicles	52	73
Budget for running costs	F2·7 millions	F8·3 millions

It will, of course, be some time before the new units are fully operational. The expansion in the mobile library network will, however, soon begin to raise book circulation figures.

At the time of the report to the interministerial committee only thirty nine metropolitan *départements* had a library service. The figure has now reached forty nine.

In the university library field, as in the public library sector, various large new libraries or extensions are under construction. The 1970 programme, alone, should add a further 50,195 square metres to the available floor space. Unfortunately, however, the final shape of this programme may well have to wait upon the large scale reorganisation of universities now in progress.

Index

Académie de Médecine Library 81
Accession registers 93
Aisne region library scheme 69
Aix-Marseilles university library 80, 82, 85
American Library School in Paris, 1923-29 100
Army libraries 60
Archives 106
Archives de France 106
Arsenal library (Bibliothèque de l'Arsenal) 17
Assises Nationales des Bibliothèques, 1968 114
Association de l'Ecole National Supérieure de Bibliothécaires 104
Association des Bibliothécaires Français 100, 103
Association des Documentalistes et des Bibliothécaires Spécialisés 104
Association des Titulaires des Diplômes Supérieurs de Bibliothécaire, 1960-67 105
Association Nationale de la Recherche Technique 107
Association Nationale des Bibliothécaires Municipaux 104
Associations Départementales de Lecture Publique 69-76

Beauvais public library 42
Besançon public library 36
Bibliothèque d'Art et d'Archéologie 22
Bibliothèque de Documentation Internationale Contemporaine 22
Bibliothèque de la Sorbonne 21

Bibliothèque des Arts Graphiques 23
Bibliothèque Finno-Scandinave 21
Bibliothèque Forney 31
Bibliothèque Historique de la Ville de Paris 25
Bibliothèque Littéraire Jacques-Doucet 21
Bibliothèque Mazarine 24
Bibliothèque Nationale 15, 16
Bibliothèque Nationale, Annexe Les Halles, proposed 17
Bibliothèque Nationale et Universitaire, Strasbourg 17, 81, 85, 86
Bibliothèques centrales de prêt 65-66, 69-76
Bibliothèques pour Tous 55-56
Bibliothèques publiques (ie, sector libraries serving 100,000 population), proposed 115
Bibliothèques régionales de prêt, proposed 115
Bleton, M, Service technique, DBLP 10
Blind, Libraries for the 60
Bookbinding 93
Book loans 92
Bordeaux public library 37
Bordeaux university library 80, 85, 86
Building programmes, public libraries, 1968-70 48-50
Building programmes, rural library headquarters, 1965-68 74
Building programmes, university libraries, 1955-71 85-89
Building standards of the DBLP, municipal central and branch libraries 50-54

117

Bulletin des bibliothèques de France 93
Bulletin d'informations, Association des Bibliothécaires Français 93, 104
Bulletin signalétique, CNRS 107

Caen university library 11, 81, 85, 86
Caen municipal library 37
CAFB (Certificat d'Aptitude aux Fonctions de Bibliothécaire) 101, 103
Cambrai public library 37
Catalogue Collectif des Ouvrages Étrangers 96
Catalogue Collectif des Périodiques du Debut du XVIIe Siècle à 1939 95, 96
Centre Laïque de lecture publique 57
Centre National de la Recherche Scientifique 107
Centres Hospitaliers et Universitaires 81, 82
Children's book awards 63
Children's libraries 61-68
' Classified ' public libraries 35-41
Classification systems 92
Clermont-Ferrand public library 38
Colmar public library 38
Comité Français de la Reprographie 108
Comité National de la Documentation Scientifique et Technique 106
Computers and data processing 94, 108
Conservatoire National de Musique 17
Conservatoire National des Arts et Métiers 108
Cooperation, Inter-library 95-97
Copyright deposit 17-18

Dennery, *M* Administrator, BN and Director of Libraries 10
Dijon university library 85
Diplomas in librarianship 98-105
Diplôme Supérieur de Bibliothécaire 101
Diplôme Technique de Bibliothécaire 101
Direction des Archives de France 106
Direction des Bibliothèques et de la Lecture Publique 9-14, 110-116
Discothèque de Paris 28
Documentation Centre for Education in Europe 108

École de Bibliothécaires, Institut Catholique de Paris 100
École de Bibliothécaires-Documentalistes 101
École des Chartes 99-100
École des Hautes Études Sociales 100
École Nationale Supérieure de Bibliothécaires 101-103
École Nationale Supérieure des Mines, library 24
École Normale Supérieure, library 24
École Polytechnique library 24
Education for librarianship 99-105

Fines for late return of books 91
Fontaine public library 42
French National Library Board *see* Direction des Bibliothèques et de la Lecture Publique

Grades, library staff 98-99
Gramophone record libraries 27

Grandes Écoles, libraries 24
Grenoble university library 80, 82, 86, 87

Henriot, M Gabriel 100
Home book loans, duration of 91
Hospital libraries 59, 60

Institut de France, library 22
Institut National des Techniques de la Documentation 108
'Instructions de 1878' code for university libraries 82, 83
Inter-library cooperation 95-97

Joie par les Livres association 62, 63

Lecture et bibliothèques (periodical) 104
Lecture Publique en France, report, 1968 110-116
Le Havre public library 38
Legal deposit 17, 18
Les Halles, proposed annexe to BN 17
Library associations 103-105
Library cooperation 95-97
Library education 98-105
Library extension activities 61-64
Library journals 93
Library profession 98-105
Library staff; professional, technical and service 98, 99
Lille public library 80, 82, 86, 87
Loi d'Orientation 1968 84
Lyons public library 34, 39, 40

Maison de Science de l'Homme, library 25
Marseilles public library 40
Marseilles science and medical libraries 80, 82, 85

Massy public library (ENSB) 43
Mazarin, Cardinal, library of 24
Médecine, Faculté de, University of Paris 81
Medical libraries 81, 82
Membership, public libraries 93
Methods, library 90-94
Mobile libraries 72-74
Mulhouse public library 40
Municipal libraries see Public libraries
Musée de l'Homme, library 23
Musée des Arts et Traditions Populaires, library 24

Nancy university library 83, 85, 87
Nanterre, law and arts library 82, 87
National and University library, Strasbourg 17
National libraries 15-19
National Library Board see Direction des Bibliothèques et de la Lecture Publique
National Library School (ENSB) 101-103

Orsay science library 80, 85, 87

Paris art libraries 22-24
Paris general and special libraries 20-28
Paris history, libraries of 24
Paris law libraries 25
Paris municipal libraries 29-33
Paris music libraries 25, 26
Paris natural history, libraries of 26
Paris parliamentary and ministerial libraries 26
Paris university libraries 21
Phonothèque Nationale 27
Poindron, M, Deputy-director of Libraries 10

Public libraries, building programmes, 1968-70 48-50
Public libraries, 'classified'
institutions 35-41
Public libraries, membership
93
Public libraries, methods 90-
94
Public libraries, standards of
accommodation 48-50
Public libraries, statistics 43-
47

Recherche technique, journal
of ANRT 107
Regional lending libraries,
proposed 115
Répertoire des Revues Tech-
niques pour l'Industrie 107
Réunion des Bibliothèques de
Paris 15
Riom public library 42
Rural libraries 65, 66, 69-76

Sainte - Geneviève library,
Paris 20, 85
Saint-Martin-d'Hères, public
library 42
Salvan, *Mlle* Paule (ENSB) 101
Sarcelles public library 42
School libraries 61-68
Secondary school libraries 65,
66
Sector libraries, proposed 115

Seine - inférieure library
scheme 69
Service Central des Prêts 97
Service des Echanges Universitaires 95
Service d'Information Bibliographique 96
Sorbonne library 21
St-Diè public library 35, 36
Statistics, public libraries in
Paris suburbs 45-47
public library provision 1965
43-45
public library provision 1968
110-111
Strasbourg, National and University library 17, 81

Teachers' libraries 67
Tours public library 41
Troyes public library 41

Union catalogues 13
Union Française des Organ-
ismes de Documentation 108
University libraries 77-89
University libraries building
programmes 1955-71 85-89
University libraries instruc-
tions of June 1962 83
University students, increase
in numbers 1914-68 78, 79

Vendel, Henri 100

Works libraries 57-59